The Tupperware Book of

PICNICS PARTIES & SNACKS AROUND THE WORLD

On the cover: Picnic-Party-Snack food from around the world—picnic from Copenhagen, party Pear Dessert from Frankfurt, Shrimp Brochette snack from Montevideo.

Back cover: Tropical Fruit Sherbets from Caracas.

The Tupperware Book of

PICNICS PARTIES & SNACKS AROUND THE WORLD

by Mary Ann Zimmerman
Photographs by William Lanyon

A Benjamin Company / Rutledge Book
distributed by
Simon & Schuster, Inc., New York

AN ESSANDESS SPECIAL EDITION

We wish to thank the following restaurants and Inter Continental Hotels for their generosity in sharing their recipes with us:

AMSTERDAM: Zuurkool Met Spek–Five Flies.

ATHENS: Moussaka, Stuffed Dolmas, Dionysus Tart, Shrimp Tassia–Dionysus.

MELBOURNE: All recipes–Hotel Southern Cross, Melbourne.

BOGOTA: Chicken Soup Tequendama Style–Hotel Tequendama; Brisket of Beef in Beer, Pork Loin Cooked in the Oven–Los Arrayanes.

BUENOS AIRES: Empanada–Pulperia "La Carcel"; Puchero–La Cabaña.

CARACAS: Tamanaco Carne Asado, Pabellon Criollo, Tostados–Hotel Tamanaco.

COPENHAGEN: All food–photographed at Illums Bolighus.

CURACAO: All recipes–Curacao Inter Continental.

DUBLIN: All recipes–Dublin Inter Continental.

LONDON: Game Pie, Scones–Savoy Hotel.

PARIS: Omelette, Eggs in Gelatin, Butter and Nut Sandwich, Roquefort and Armagnac Sandwich, Tarte of 4 Fruits–Fauchon; French hors d'oeuvres–Chez Raffatin et Honorine; Roast Filet of Lamb–Relais Louis XIII.

FRANKFURT: All recipes–Frankfurt Inter Continental.

HONG KONG: All recipes except picnic–The Mandarin Hotel.

ROME: Chocolato Tartufo–Tre Scalini.

BEIRUT: All recipes–Hotel Phoenicia Inter Continental.

LIMA: Peruvian Causa–La Ronda; Suspiro Lemiño–La Calesa; Duck Cuzco, Lamb Las Trece Monedas –Las Trece Monedas; Mixed Anticucho–La Fonda del Sol, N.Y.C.

MANILA: Pork Adobo, Pancit, Palabok–Bon Vivant; all Merienda recipes–The Luau.

PUERTO RICO: SAN JUAN Pineapple Bombay.

RIO de JANEIRO: Brazilian Mixed Grill on Skewer–La Fonda del Sol, N.Y.C.; Picadinho–Casa Brasil, N.Y.C.

SINGAPORE: All recipes–Hotel Singapura Inter Continental.

GENEVA: Cheese and Onion Tartlet with White Wine, Minced Veal Geneva Inter Continental, Hotel Inter Continental Geneva.

TAIPEI: All recipes–The Grand Hotel.

BANGKOK: All recipes–Hotel Siam Inter Continental.

TOKYO: Sukiyaki Okura, Tempura, Yakitori, Teppan-Yaki–Hotel Okura; Mitzutaki–Hogetsudo Restaurant.

MONTEVIDEO: All recipes–Victoria Plaza Hotel.

SOUTH AMERICAN PARRILLADA: Grilled Latin American Sausages–La Fonda del Sol, N.Y.C.

Prepared and produced by Rutledge Books, Inc.
Library of Congress Catalog Card Number 67–21951

Printed in the United States of America
Published by The Benjamin Company, Inc.
485 Madison Avenue, New York, New York 10022
Simultaneously published in Canada.

Distributed by
Simon & Schuster, Inc., New York

CONTENTS

Pronunciation Guide 7
Introduction 8
Athens 9
Amsterdam 14
Copenhagen 20
Dublin 25
Frankfurt 27
Geneva 32
London 36
Paris 41
Rome 46
Beirut 53
Melbourne 59
Bangkok 64
Hong Kong 68
Manila 78
Singapore 83
Taipei 89
Tokyo 93
San Juan (Puerto Rico) 99
Willemstad (Curacao) 102
South American Parrillada 107
Caracas 110
Lima 113
Montevideo 118
Bogota 123
Rio 126
Buenos Aires 129
Picnic Guide 132
Recipe Index 140

To Eddie
and our boys . . .
Michael, Peter and Chris

HOW DO YOU PRONOUNCE IT?

ATHENS

Avgolemono Soupa . . . av-go-lemon-o

Dionysus Tart . . . dion-e-sos

Moussaka . . . moo-sa-ka

Shrimp Tassia . . . tas-see-a

Stuffed Dolmas . . . dole-mas

Tarama . . . tar-a-ma

AMSTERDAM

Zuurkool . . . zeer-coal

BEIRUT

Habash Mahshi . . . hab-bash mah-she

Hummus Bi Taheeni . . . homus b ta-he-nee

Kabiss . . . ka-bes

Karabeej . . . kar-a-beej

Katayef . . . ka-tie-yief

Moudardara . . . moo-jad-dara

Tabbouleh . . . ta-boo-lee

BANGKOK

Kaeng Phed . . . kang ped

Kung Nao . . . koog now

Pu Cha . . . poo cha

MANILA

Lumpia . . . lum-pia

Palabok . . . pal-a-book

Pancit . . . pan-sit

Pork Adobo . . . a-doe-bo

Ukoy . . . oo-coy

TOKYO

Mitzutaki . . . met-zoo-ta-kee

Onigiri . . . on-e-gear-e

Sukiyaki . . . sue-kee-a-kee

Sushi . . . sue-she

Tempura . . . temp-por-a

Yakitori . . . yak-e-tor-e

CURACAO

Cala . . . cal-a

Keshy Yena . . . kesh-e yena

Kesita . . . kes-e-ta

Pastechi . . . pas-ta-kee

CARACAS

Bienmesabe . . . bee-en-mes-a-bee

Carne Asada . . . car-nee a-sa-da

Pabellon . . . pa-bay-yon

Tostados . . . tos-ta-dos

LIMA

Mixed Anticucho . . . an-tee-cu-cho

Peruvian Causa . . . ca-sa

BOGOTA

Brisket of Beef Sobrebarriga . . . so-bray-ba-re-ga

Lomo de Cerdo . . . lo-mo day cer-do

MONTEVIDEO

Chaja . . . cha-ha

Asado con Cuero Chimichurria . . . a-sa-do con kuay-roe che-me-chur-ria

Carbonada Criollo . . . car-bon-a-da cre-ol-ja

Shrimp Brochette with Sauce Aioli . . . ah-yo-lee

RIO

Papos deAnjo . . . pap-pos de an-joe

BUENOS AIRES

Empanada . . . em-pan-a-da

Puchero . . . poo-chair-o

About a year and a half ago, I approached Tupperware Home Parties, Orlando, Florida, manufacturers of all types of plastic food containers, with an idea for a cookbook.

I envisioned a different type of book—one that would, with recipes and pictures, not only bring to life the exciting international food but also the environment in which we found it. I would not attempt to cover the entire cuisine of each country but would limit my tasting to specific food categories: Picnics, Parties, Snacks.

Last September, armed with two suitcases of Tupperware and an around-the-world itinerary that covered 25 countries, photographer Bill Lanyon and I set out to explore the world of good food.

We photographed Tupperware in food situations wherever it would be appropriate for use as a serving or storage container. Then recipes were written to fit into specific containers—for ease of recognition, the names of these containers have been capitalized. It only stands to reason that if you're taking the time to prepare a delicious dish, proper storage of the food is essential. Freezer information is also given where it pertains, to take advantage of cooking ahead.

I would like to pay special homage to all the Tupperware people around the world who were so unselfishly cooperative and, in the United States, my special gratitude to the Tupperware staff at International Headquarters in Orlando, Florida. To Ruth Ziegel, the home economist who did such a superb job of testing all the recipes—my heartfelt thanks.

This book has been written for both the traveler and the non-traveler. The stay-at-home cook will be taken on an armchair culinary odyssey that covers some 49,000 miles. Illustrations are used to give the "flavor" of the food as well as the country.

For the traveler who doesn't cook—and wouldn't dream of any cooking experience more rarefied than opening a can—this book can be used as a bird's-eye guide of what dishes to eat all over the world.

The traveler who loves to eat and cook will be delighted to find old favorites and new dishes to try. The time span in each country was all too brief, but we believe we have selected many of the most interesting specialties from each country—specialties that the average tourist has time to try. By all means, try our suggestions—but be adventurous too, and discover some of your own favorites. Bringing home the recipe for a dish you have enjoyed (or using ours) will help relive that pleasure again and again.

Mary Ann Zimmerman

ATHENS

First stop on our culinary odyssey is Athens, a city with two distinct heartbeats, both of them exciting. On the one hand, there's the majesty of magnificent ancient ruins; on the other, Athens has the gay ambience of a rollicking Mediterranean resort. The Parthenon, the architectural marvel that so proudly dominates the city, is appropriately every tourist's first stop. Next, visit the restaurant just opposite the Parthenon to enjoy at leisure your first sampling of Greek food favorites.

PICNICS

Greece, with its variety of beaches, boat and land excursions, is a picnicker's paradise. Here, as in every country visited, we tried to come away with new approaches for picnicking anywhere in the U.S.A. Why not vary your picnic routine with Orektikon or Peasant Salad? The Peasant Salad looks prettier when you use a Party Susan to keep the ingredients separate.

Above, Superb Greek food: Dionysus Tart, Moussaka, Stuffed Vine Leaves.

AVGOLEMONO SOUP

Serves 8

8 cups chicken stock
1/3 cup white rice
Kufta (meatballs—recipe below)
1 teaspoon dehydrated parsley flakes
5 tablespoons lemon juice
2 egg yolks

Bring stock to boil in large saucepan. Add rice and Kufta. Simmer covered 20 minutes. Add parsley. Combine lemon juice and yolks, beat thoroughly. Add 1 cup soup gradually to yolk-juice mixture, stirring constantly. Return to soup and simmer, stirring constantly, until egg is cooked, about 1 minute. Serve at once.

This soup is great cold. Don't heat after adding yolks, but remove to Fix-N-Mix and cool at once; then soup will not be too thick when cold. Avgolemono Soup is often served after Orektikon.

KUFTA

28 tiny meatballs

½ pound ground lamb
¼ pound ground beef
¼ cup dry bread crumbs
1 egg yolk
1 small onion, finely minced
1 teaspoon salt
½ teaspoon pepper
¼ teaspoon allspice
2 tablespoons chopped parsley
1 tablespoon cooking oil

Combine all ingredients, except oil. Form into tiny balls, the size of large marbles. Use wet hands to make balls more easily. Heat oil and add meatballs. Cook over low heat until done. Drain well and add to soup. Store in a Square Round until used.

These freeze beautifully; can also be served hot as appetizers.

PARTIES

The Greek equivalent of French hors d'oeuvres or Italian antipasto is Orektikon. Use these Greek tidbits to add zest to your favorite kind of party—a cocktail buffet, a picnic, or a summer luncheon. One Piraeus restaurant serves 19 varieties, including: clams, olives, blue cheese, anchovies, head cheese, stuffed vine leaves, tiny fish, fried shrimp. Recipes for some Orektikon, and Moussaka, one of the most popular Greek party recipes, follow.

SHRIMP CHOW CHOW

Serves 8

2 cans (2¾ ounces each) small shrimp
3 tablespoons cooked carrot, sliced and quartered
2 tablespoons chow chow sauce
2 tablespoons chopped chow chow vegetables
¼ teaspoon salt

Combine ingredients. Serve very cold on toast rounds. Store in a 2-cup Wonderlier until ready to serve.

DIONYSUS TART

Serves 6

¾ cup light cream
2 eggs, lightly beaten
½ pound Feta cheese, drained and crumbled
2 cups chopped, cooked ham (about ½ pound)
2 cups chopped, cooked chicken
1 can (4 ounces) mushrooms, drained and chopped
2 sheets phyllo pastry

Combine cream and egg until well blended. Add cheese, ham, chicken and mushrooms, mix well. Line a 10-inch pie pan with half phyllo, pour in filling. Fit another sheet of phyllo on top. Trim edges and turn top crust under bottom crust, pinch to seal. Cut into 6 portions before baking. Bake in 350°F. oven for 50 minutes (center will be slightly runny). If top browns before pie is baked, cover with foil.

The pastry can be bought in leaves at any Greek store—it is impossible for anyone but a Greek grandmother to make it at home.

SHRIMPS TASSIA

Serves 6

4 tablespoons butter
2½ pounds shrimp, shelled and deveined
1 cup sliced fresh mushrooms
2 onions, finely chopped (1 cup)
1 small carrot, finely chopped
1 clove garlic, minced
2 sprigs parsley
1 bay leaf
¼ teaspoon thyme
3 tablespoons ketchup
1 cup dry white wine
¼ cup warmed brandy
¼ cup heavy cream
croutons

Melt butter in large skillet, add shrimp, mushrooms and ½ cup chopped onion. Sauté over moderate heat until shrimp are pink and onions wilted. Transfer to a warm dish. Add remaining vegetables to skillet, sauté until slightly soft. Add bay leaf, thyme, ketchup and wine. Cover and simmer 30 minutes. Add shrimp to sauce and bring to a simmer. Add warm brandy and flambé. When flame goes out, stir in heavy cream. Heat thoroughly and serve garnished with croutons.

MOUSSAKA

Serves 8 to 10

3 medium eggplants, cut into ½-inch slices
½ cup olive oil
3 onions, chopped
2 pounds ground lamb
3 tablespoons tomato paste
1 teaspoon salt
⅛ teaspoon basil
6 tablespoons butter
6 tablespoons flour
3 cups milk, heated
3 eggs, beaten
½ cup bread crumbs
½ cup grated Parmesan cheese

Spread eggplant slices in a large roasting pan. Sprinkle with ¼ cup olive oil. Cover with foil and bake in 350°F. oven 30 minutes. Remove and set aside. Heat remaining oil in large skillet. Add onion, sauté until tender. Add lamb and cook until brown. Add tomato paste, salt and basil; simmer uncovered over low heat until all liquid is absorbed. Melt butter in saucepan, add flour and stir to blend. Cook over low heat 2 to 3 minutes. Gradually add milk, stirring constantly. Cook over low heat until mixture is thickened and smooth. Remove from heat. Add a little hot mixture to beaten eggs, beating constantly. Add remaining white sauce, stirring rapidly to prevent egg from cooking. Sprinkle the bottom of a 3-quart casserole with bread crumbs, cover with a layer of eggplant, then a layer of lamb mixture, repeating until both mixtures are used up. Pour white sauce over all and sprinkle with cheese. Bake, uncovered, in 375°F. oven 1 hour, or until casserole is golden and fluffy.

This is a delicious party dish with a subtle blend of flavors. It's as pretty to look at as it is good to eat.

TARAMA

1¾ cups

6 slices trimmed white bread
1 4-ounce jar (about ½ cup) codfish roe
6 tablespoons lemon juice
1 egg yolk
¼ cup olive oil

Soak bread in cold water. Combine roe, lemon juice and yolk; beat until well blended. Squeeze water out of bread and add to roe mixture, beating constantly. Add oil gradually, beating constantly. Beat until smooth. Store in 2-cup Wonderlier until ready to use. Serve with Arabic flat bread. Can be garnished with green pepper, tomatoes and Greek olives if desired.

SNACKS

Nothing will ever replace hamburgers as the Number One American Snack. That's no reason not to snack native style wherever you travel. We know of no better way to enjoy the tempo of a city than mixing with the local people as they stop for a light bite at snack bar or sidewalk café. Many of the best snack recipes unearthed in our tasting around the world can be classified as open sandwiches. A favorite is Greek Souvlakia.

SOUVLAKIA (SKEWERED LAMB)

Serves 8 as hors d'oeuvre

1 pound leg of lamb cut into 1-inch cubes
lemon juice
salt
pepper
paprika
oregano
Arabic Bread (recipe below)
Yoghurt Sauce (recipe below)

Dip lamb cubes in lemon juice and place on skewers. Season with salt, pepper, paprika and a dash of oregano. Cook over charcoal or under broiler, turning occasionally, until browned on all sides but not dried. Serve with Arabic Flat Bread and Yoghurt Sauce.

YOGHURT SAUCE

1½ cups

1 cucumber
1 cup plain yoghurt
1 tablespoon olive oil
2 teaspoons vinegar
½ teaspoon salt
4 cloves garlic, pressed

Peel cucumber and remove seeds; grate and drain excess liquid. Combine with remaining ingredients and stir until completely combined.

FLAT BREAD

Makes 12

1 package (13¾ ounce) hot roll mix
¼ cup coarse crystal salt

Prepare hot roll mix according to package directions. After rising, place on floured board and knead lightly. Divide into 12 even pieces. Roll out each piece to 6-inch diameter. Place 2 on each of 6 ungreased cookie sheets. Prick thoroughly with a fork. Sprinkle lightly with salt. Bake in 400°F. oven 5 to 6 minutes or until golden, slightly bubbly on surface, and crisp.

STUFFED VINE LEAVES

Makes 70

1 quart jar grape leaves
1 pound ground beef or lamb
3 large onions, chopped
1 cup rice
¼ cup chopped parsley
¼ cup butter
1 cup lemon juice
2½ cups beef bouillon
3 eggs, beaten

Wash leaves, separate and place shiny side down. Sauté meat, onions, rice and parsley in butter until meat is brown and onions soft. Place about 1 teaspoon of meat mixture on each leaf. Starting at base of leaf fold over meat mixture; next fold sides over and roll tightly toward tip. Arrange rolls in large saucepan. Sprinkle with lemon juice and ½ bouillon. Place a plate over rolls to weight them down. Simmer, covered, 25 minutes. Add remaining bouillon and simmer another 35 minutes. Remove from heat and place stuffed leaves in Cold Cut Keeper. Add hot liquid, a little at a time, to beaten eggs, beating constantly. Return egg mixture to heat, and cook over low heat until mixture starts to thicken. Cool slightly. Pour over leaves and store covered in refrigerator until ready to serve. May be kept several days in a Cold Cut Keeper.

Excellent flavor — a very good "dolma" recipe.

Peasant Salad: lettuce, shredded cabbage, Feta, olives, scallions, anchovies, oregano.

Amsterdam

Go to Holland prepared to eat heartily. The Dutch boast of their eating prowess and concede that they eat all day. You'll want to do the same! Start with an enormous breakfast of meat, cheese, bread, peanut butter, jelly, cocoa or tea. "Elevenses," equivalent to our coffee break, comes next. Then time for lunch—the famous Dutch Coffee Table—and you're only halfway through the day. No matter—even if you can't fit into your clothes, you'll enjoy the Dutch stick-to-your-ribs fare.

PICNICS

A Dutch Coffee Table usually contains 3 different kinds of bread, cheese and meat. It requires little advance preparation and is, therefore, particularly adapted to a spur-of-the-moment urge to get up and go. Take along a Snack-Stor filled with your picnic. At home you'll find many Dutch products in your supermarket so you can approximate a Coffee Table.

DUTCH KOFFIE TAFEL (COFFEE TABLE)

Breads: Rozijnenbrood (raisin bread), Ontbijtkoek (brown breakfast cake) Knaekebrod (crisp Norwegian bread), white bread, brown bread (cracked wheat), Broodjes or Cadetjes (soft white rolls), Krentebroodjes (currant bread), rusk.

Cheeses: Leidsekaas (Dutch Leyden cheese), Edam, Gouda, Farmer cheese.

Meats: Boiled ham, Rookvlees (a salty spiced beef), roast beef, pâté.

Sweets: Two kinds of jam; Muisjes (little mice) — similar to anise — sprinkled on buttered white bread and eaten for dessert; Speculaas (a cookie), and chocolate sprinkles — both eaten on buttered bread.

BITTERBALLEN

Makes 60

3 tablespoons butter
4 tablespoons flour
1 cup milk
2 cups chopped cooked meat (roast beef, veal or ham or a combination of all three)
1 tablespoon minced parsley
1 teaspoon salt
1 teaspoon worcestershire sauce
1/8 teaspoon pepper
3/4 cup fine, dry unseasoned bread crumbs
1 egg
2 tablespoons water
oil

Melt butter, blend in flour. Slowly add milk, blending until smooth. Cook over low heat, stirring constantly, until sauce is thick, about 5 minutes. Mix sauce, meat, parsley, salt, worcestershire sauce and pepper. Wet hands and shape mixture into 1/2-inch balls. Roll in crumbs and let dry for 2 hours. Mix egg with water. Dip balls in egg and again in bread crumbs. Pour oil into fry pan to depth of 1 1/2 inches. Heat to 400°F. (hot) and fry until golden—1 or 2 minutes. Drain and serve at once. If desired these may be frozen in 2-quart Wonderlier uncooked, separated with layers of freezer paper. To serve, thaw and fry as above.

Very good hot appetizer with creamy center and interesting flavor. Make them bite-size to be served as finger food.

PARTIES

Try pancakes for parties. Served the Dutch way, pancakes make marvelous eating any time of day. Dutch pancakes are huge, at least the size of a 10-inch skillet. Serve Rusk Pancakes for dessert, Meat-Filled Pancakes as a Sunday supper and Apple or Bacon Pancakes at a leisurely brunch. For easy entertaining, cook ahead and freeze. Our other Party recipes are typically Dutch, eaten in Amsterdam and adapted for your kitchen.

MEAT-FILLED PANCAKE

Serves 4

1 cup flour
1 1/2 cups milk
2 eggs
1/2 teaspoon salt
2 tablespoons butter
Meat Filling (recipe below)

Measure flour into medium mixing bowl, add milk and blend thoroughly. Add eggs and salt, beat until smooth. Store until ready to use (batter will keep two or three days). To prepare pancakes, melt 1 tablespoon butter in 10-inch skillet, pour in half the batter. Brown pancake well on one side, turn and brown lightly on the other side. Keep hot while preparing the second pancake. Spread filling on light side of first pancake and turn second pancake, brown side up, on top of first. Cut into wedges and serve at once.

MEAT FILLING

¼ cup butter
6 tablespoons flour
2 cups bouillon or stock
½ teaspoon salt
⅛ teaspoon pepper
½ teaspoon nutmeg
2 tablespoons lemon juice
2 cups cooked meat, ground or minced (about 1 pound)
1 4-ounce can mushrooms, drained (about ½ cup)

Melt butter, blend in flour. Slowly add bouillon, stirring constantly, until mixture is smooth. Cook over low heat, stirring occasionally until thick, about 8 minutes. Add seasonings, meat and mushrooms. Keep meat hot while preparing pancakes, or store in 2-quart Wonderlier until ready to use.

EVERYDAY PANCAKES

6 large cakes

1 package active dry yeast
¼ cup warm water
4 cups warm milk
4 cups flour
1 teaspoon salt
butter

Dissolve yeast in warm water, add to warm milk. Combine flour and salt in large mixing bowl; gradually stir in liquids, beating until smooth. Let rise 45 minutes. Lightly grease a 12-inch skillet; when very hot pour on about ¾ cup batter. Tilt pan quickly to cover bottom with batter. Brown lightly on one side, turn and brown quickly on other side. Serve with sugar or molasses.

APPLE PANCAKES

Prepare batter as above. When batter is poured, place 4 or 5 slices of peeled apple on batter. Brown lightly and turn carefully to brown other side. Serve with brown sugar, butter and cinnamon.

BACON PANCAKES

Prepare batter as above. Place 3 or 4 slices of crisp cooked bacon on bottom of skillet with a little bacon fat and butter. Cover with batter and cook until brown. Turn carefully and brown other side. Serve with brown sugar or molasses.

These pancakes are also very tasty when cooked like the very thin Breton crêpe. . . . They freeze well and can be frozen and stacked in the Pie Taker. Stacked cakes should be separated with freezer paper.

REAL HOLLAND PANCAKES

Makes 3 large pancakes

1 cup flour
½ teaspoon salt
2 large eggs, beaten
1 cup milk
⅓ cup butter

Measure flour and salt into medium-size mixing bowl. Add eggs and half the milk; beat until smooth. Add remaining milk to make a thin batter. Cover and set aside about two hours. Melt 2 tablespoons of the butter in a large skillet and add just enough batter to cover bottom of pan. Turn pancakes frequently, each time adding butter. They should then become golden brown and crisp at the sides. Serve with melted butter, syrup or cooked fruit.

RUSK PANCAKE

Serves 4

3 eggs
¼ cup sugar
1 teaspoon vanilla extract
1 cup milk
3 tablespoons butter
4 Holland rusks
confectioners sugar or rum

Beat eggs with sugar and vanilla, add milk slowly, beating constantly. Melt butter in large skillet, add rusks. Pour most of egg mixture over rusks and slowly brown over low heat. Gradually add remaining liquid until absorbed by rusks. Turn pancake and brown on other side. Sprinkle with sugar or rum and serve at once.

ZUURKOOL MET SPEK

Serves 4 to 5

1 pound 11-ounce can sauerkraut (about 4 cups)
4 slices bacon, half cooked
1½ pounds potatoes, mashed (about 3 cups mashed)
½ pound smoked sausage, sliced

Place sauerkraut in 8-cup frypan and place bacon on top. Cover and simmer 20 minutes. Remove from heat and drain excess sauerkraut juice. Place heated sauerkraut on one side of pan and cover with cooked bacon. Place mashed potatoes on other side of pan and cover with sausage slices. Cover and cook over moderate heat about 5 minutes or until sausage and potatoes are thoroughly heated. Serve at once.

MOCK POTATO ROLLS

Serves 8 to 10

2 pounds potatoes
¼ cup chopped cooked ham
2 tablespoons butter
2 teaspoons tomato paste
½ teaspoon salt
¼ teaspoon pepper
6 tablespoons butter

Cook potatoes, peel and mash. Combine with remaining ingredients and beat until well blended. Place in a 4-cup Wonderlier, chill at least one hour. Just before serving remove from refrigerator and shape into 16 balls, about 1½ inches in diameter. Melt butter in large frypan. Heat until bubbly but not brown. Drop balls into butter and brown well on all sides. Serve at once.

SNACKS

The Dutch have many favorites. In summer, it's raw herring sold by pushcart vendors. In the winter, something hot to counteract the frosty weather. When it freezes, half of Holland becomes a skating rink with canals thronged with people. Snack bars are set up at such places as Marken, 20 minutes from Amsterdam. Here you'll find currant bread, hot chocolate, hot anise milk and Holland's legendary Pea Soup.

POTATO-CHEESE SOUFFLE

Serves 8

2 pounds potatoes
1 cup hot milk
¼ cup soft butter
1 teaspoon salt
⅛ teaspoon ground pepper
¼ teaspoon ground nutmeg
1 cup grated Gouda cheese
3 eggs, separated

Cook potatoes; peel and whip until smooth and fluffy. Blend in milk, butter, salt, pepper, nutmeg, cheese and egg yolks. Beat until light and fluffy. Beat egg whites until stiff but not dry. Fold into potato mixture. Spoon soufflé into an unbuttered 8-cup casserole. Bake in a 350°F. oven 45 to 50 minutes or until soufflé is puffed up and top is brown. Serve at once.

PEA SOUP

4 quarts soup

2 cups green split peas (about 1 pound)
3½ cups cold water
1 tablespoon salt
2 pig's feet
1½ cups chopped celery
1¼ cups chopped leeks (3 large)
½ pound smoked sausage, cubed or coarsely sliced

Soak peas in 3 cups of cold water (in 2-quart Wonderlier) 12 hours. Drain and add enough water to make 3½ quarts. Add salt and bring to a boil. Skim; add pig's feet, celery and leeks. Simmer, covered, 4 or 5 hours, or until pig's feet are quite tender and meat loosens from the bone. Lift out pig's feet and discard skin and bones. Add bits of meat to soup. Half an hour before serving add smoked sausage. Strips of toasted bread and dark pumpernickel are served with this soup.

The soup flavor improves upon standing and should be made at least 1 day before serving . . . Store in a Fix-N-Mix bowl or freeze half and store half to serve next day.

DUTCH FRIED EGGS

Serves 3

5 tablespoons butter
6 very thin slices white bread
12 slices (½ pound) ham or roast beef
salt
pepper
mustard pickles

Spread all the bread slices with butter, using 2 tablespoons for the 6 slices. Place 2 slices of meat on each slice of bread. Fry eggs in remaining 3 tablespoons butter, cooking until set but not hard. Place an egg on each slice of bread, serve 2 per person. Serve with salt, pepper and garnish with pickles.

Even picnics ride bikes in Amsterdam.

holland

PICNIC

Copenhagen

It's impossible to think of Copenhagen without thinking of its food. There is an abundance of good things to eat, beautifully prepared and displayed as artfully as if the cook were artist putting oil to canvas. You're bound to become a smorrebrod fancier and to gorge yourself on Danish pastries. It is the delicious Danish open sandwiches, however — no relation to our own sandwiches — that should become a permanent part of your menus. Use them for Picnics, Parties, Snacks.

PICNICS

Using Tupperware, Danish open sandwiches become transportable and a great idea for picnicking. Butter slices of a variety of breads, carry in Bread Server. Place different fillings, salads and garnishes from our listing in individual Cereal Bowls and Small Square Rounds. You can even take raw eggs to be used to top tartar steak. Everyone concocts his own sandwich.

COPENHAGEN SALAD

5 cups salad

½ pound Samsoe cheese cut into ½-inch cubes
3 apples, peeled, cored and diced (4½ cups)
¾ cup cooked peas
4 slices bacon, cooked and diced
2 ounces smoked sausage, cut in cubes
2 tablespoons oil
1 tablespoon lemon juice
1 teaspoon sugar
1 teaspoon prepared mustard

Combine ingredients in 2-quart Wonderlier. Marinate at least 1 hour before serving.

More or less Copenhagen's answer to our Waldorf Salad, but this one is much heartier with the addition of cheese, bacon and sausage. The dressing is sharp but smooth, and the peas add color.

PARTIES

For dessert, cold Buttermilk Soup and Cornets with Whipped Cream are delicious ways to end a Danish party. Start your party using Danish table appointments, expertly designed modern ceramics and woodenware. Copy, if you can, the Danes' great knack for unusual table settings combining imagination, an unhackneyed color sense, a flair for making the ordinary unique. Their decorative ways with napkins are marvelous.

CORNETS WITH WHIPPED CREAM

12 Cornets

2 eggs
½ cup sugar
1 cup sifted flour
⅓ cup butter, melted
1½ cups sweetened whipped cream
strawberry jam

Beat eggs until thick and lemon colored. Add sugar gradually, beating well after each addition. Beat until light and fluffy. Add flour and butter to egg mixture, starting and ending with flour. Beat at medium speed 10 minutes. Roll out to about ⅛-inch thickness on floured board. Cut in 5-inch rounds. Cut out 5-inch

Smorrebrod can go to picnics, too—ingredients can easily be organized.

Cornets with Whipped Cream.

rounds of aluminum foil and place cookie rounds on them. Bake three at a time in a 425°F. oven four minutes. Working in open oven with rack pulled out, pick up one cookie at a time, peel off foil and roll immediately to form cone shape. Stick with toothpick to hold shape, and let cool. If cookie hardens before shaped, return to oven for a few seconds to soften. Grease hands while rolling cookies or work with glove-type pot holders, since cookies must be shaped while very hot. When all cookies are shaped and cooled, fill with whipped cream and garnish with strawberry jam. If desired, cookies may be filled and frozen —remove from freezer 30 minutes before serving. To freeze, place filled cookies on flat baking sheet and freeze until solid. Remove and place in two layers in Jumbo Bread Server. Place foil or plastic wrap between layers to separate.

COLD BUTTERMILK SOUP

Serves 6

2 egg yolks
⅓ cup sugar
1 quart buttermilk
1 teaspoon lemon juice
1 cup heavy cream, whipped
1 cup blanched, slivered almonds
strawberry jam

Beat egg yolks until thick and lemon colored. Beat in sugar a little at a time, beating well between additions. Fold in buttermilk and lemon juice. Pour into 2-quart Wonderlier, refrigerate until ready to serve. Serve icy cold garnished with whipped cream, nuts and strawberry jam.

This is absolutely one of the best cold soups I have tasted. It is refreshing and the flavor is amazing—tart yet creamy rich.

SNACKS

For after anything — a summer concert, an exhausting game of tennis, a cooling swim — serve Danish open sandwiches. Place sample "models" of from 8 to 10 varieties of open sandwiches at the top of your table. Components, in individual Square Rounds, go underneath the "models" so guests may follow your lead or concoct their own. For snacking, use miniature-size breads. Serve larger sandwiches with knife and fork.

Buttermilk Soup.

SMORREBROD

There are three major components of the Danish open sandwich and all three must complement each other in taste and appearance:

1. Bread, either dark or white, plus butter. Be sure butter completely covers the bread.
2. Next layer can be fish, meat, salad, etc.
3. Finally, the garnish.

In eating these sandwiches, one starts with the fish, proceeds to meats and salads, and ends with cheeses. Your sandwiches must have a harmony of taste and be a pleasure to the eye. We have listed some possible combinations in this order:

FISH

Smoked Eel and Scrambled Eggs: Strips of smoked eel fillet on buttered rye bread—top with cold scrambled eggs, garnish with chives.

Shrimps and Lemon: Arrange

miniature Danish shrimps (as many as 50 or 60) on buttered white bread in a pyramid—serve with lemon twists and freshly ground pepper.

Sardines in Tomato Sauce: Brisling sardines in tomato sauce are arranged to cover buttered brown bread — top with a strip of mayonnaise, garnish with twisted lemon slices, paper thin.

Smoked Salmon and Caviar: A small leaf of Bibb lettuce, smoked salmon on top of buttered white bread — top with Danish caviar, garnish with asparagus tip.

Herring and Raw Egg: Strips of smoked herring fillets on buttered rye bread — leave some space in the middle for an onion ring; place a raw egg yolk in the onion ring and pile raw onions or chopped radishes at both sides of the yolk. (Always slide raw egg yolk onto sandwiches from a spoon.)

MEATS AND SALADS

Ham and Fried Egg: Top buttered brown bread with ham sliced as thick as the bread; a fried egg goes on top of the ham — garnish with watercress, a triangle of tomato.

Ham with Peas and Carrots: Slice of ham on buttered rye bread — top with mayonnaise garnished with peas and diced carrots, crown with a sprig of watercress.

Chicken or Roast Veal and Cucumber Salad: Grilled chicken on buttered brown bread — top with cucumber salad, garnish with red currant jelly.

Roast Beef and Onion: Roast beef on buttered brown bread — top with onions browned in butter and seasoned with salt and sugar so they become crisp; garnish with piccalilli and mayonnaise.

Liver Pâté and Meat Jelly: Liver pâté on buttered brown bread, top with meat jelly, garnish with salt veal.

Liver Pâté and Bacon: Thick slice of liver pâté on buttered brown bread — top with thin rashers of Danish bacon, garnish with sliced mushrooms, salt and pepper.

Roast Pork: Roast pork on buttered brown bread—garnish with pickled cucumber cut in oblongs or prunes, apples, red cabbage. (Peeled apples are boiled until tender in sugared water; prunes are placed in a dish, boiling water is poured over them.)

Tartar: Raw minced beef on white toast — top with onion ring and raw egg yolk, garnish with capers and raw chopped onion.

CHEESES

Blue Cheese and Grapes: Danish blue cheese on buttered white toast rounds — garnish with blue grapes.

Blue Cheese and Egg Yolk: Danish blue cheese on buttered white bread — make an indentation in the center and place a raw yolk of egg inside the well, garnish with long slices of radish. When eating the sandwich, break the egg yolk and spread it evenly over the cheese.

Camembert: Camembert on buttered white toast — garnish with radishes, Spanish pepper and grapes.

The first-time visitor to Ireland has not too difficult a problem. We are already so familiar with Ireland through its folklore and lively music that we know exactly what we want to see. The musts include a tour of the lakes of Killarney through the Irish countryside with its whitewashed, thatched-roof cottages. In Dublin, it's a visit to the Abbey Theatre to see plays by Irish authors on Irish life. Shopping, look for Donegal tweeds, Waterford glass, lace, handknit sweaters.

PARTIES

So many Irish specialties — Irish stew, roast beef, corned beef and cabbage — superb as they are, have already been adopted by Americans. Recipes for these Irish dishes can be found everywhere. Our Peach Embassy is not indigenous to Ireland, but first tasted there: a luscious combination of rice, whipped cream and diced fruits, topped off with a delicate Grand Marnier Sauce.

IRISH SEAFOOD COCKTAIL DUBLIN INTER CONTINENTAL

2¼ cups sauce

1 pint mayonnaise
2 tablespoons ketchup
2 tablespoons heavy cream
1 tablespoon brandy

Blend ingredients and store in a 3-cup Wonderlier. Serve over any shellfish.

Above: Against a background of Dublin's Law Courts— two versions of delicious Peach Embassy.

PEACH EMBASSY

Serves 8 to 10

1 cup rice
2 quarts water
2 cups milk, boiled
¾ cup sugar
⅛ teaspoon salt
3 tablespoons butter
2 slices orange rind
1 teaspoon vanilla extract
½ cup chopped glacéed fruits (cherries, angelica, orange peel)
2 tablespoons apricot jam
1 cup whipped cream
English Custard (recipe below)
Grand Marnier Sauce (recipe below)

Wash rice, cover with water and bring to a boil. Drain at once. Combine with boiled milk, sugar, salt, butter, orange rind and vanilla extract. Place in 2-quart ovenproof casserole. Bring mixture to boil over medium heat. Remove from heat, cover and bake in 325°F. oven 20 to 25 minutes, or until rice is cooked and liquid absorbed. Remove from oven and remove orange peel. Cool slightly, stir in chopped fruits and jam, stirring until jam is completely melted. Cool to room temperature. Fold in English Custard and whipped cream. Pour into Bread Server, decorate with peach halves and more whipped cream. Serve with Grand Marnier Sauce.

ENGLISH CUSTARD

¼ cup sugar
2 teaspoons cornstarch
1⅓ cups milk
1 tablespoon butter or margarine
4 egg yolks
1 teaspoon vanilla extract
⅓ cup heavy cream

Combine sugar and cornstarch in medium-size saucepan. Gradually add milk, stirring until smooth. Add butter; cook over medium heat, stirring constantly, until mixture is thickened and comes to a boil. Boil 1 minute, remove from heat. Beat egg yolks slightly in medium-size bowl. Gradually add a little hot milk mixture. Cook over medium heat, stirring constantly, until mixture is thickened and comes to a boil. Boil 1 minute, remove from heat. Gradually add a little hot milk mixture, beating constantly. Stir into remaining hot mixture. Cook over medium heat, stirring constantly just until mixture boils. Remove from heat; stir in vanilla. Strain custard into 2-cup Wonderlier, refrigerate until cool. Stir in cream.

GRAND MARNIER SAUCE

2 cups apricot jam (2 12-oz. jars)
1 cup orange juice
½ cup raspberry jam
3 tablespoons Grand Marnier

Combine apricot jam, orange juice and raspberry jam in a saucepan. Cook over moderate heat until jams are completely dissolved. Add Grand Marnier and simmer 1 minute more. Remove from heat and sieve. Store in 4-cup Wonderlier until ready to use.

Rice pudding is creamy, very rich and particularly good with the diced fruits. The sauce could be bottled and sold on its own merit! A really excellent, elegant dessert.

Take a variety of German sausage on a no-cooking picnic.

Frankfurt

Frankfurt-on-Main has all the hustle and bustle of one of our big industrial cities. The river Main winds through the city, and provides a constantly changing vista of commercial river traffic. In Frankfurt, as expected, we ate our fill of German sausages and such national dishes as sauerbraten—but we were treated also to some of the finest continental food we've ever tasted, all expertly prepared and imaginatively presented by the chef at the Frankfurt Inter Continental.

PICNICS

No-cooking picnic, German style, starts with a wide variety of sausages. Our picture includes salami, bierwurst, sulze, blutschwartenmagen. Take several kinds of dark breads, mustards, a Radish Salad. An oversize cutting board could take the place of our sausage rack. Imagination and care in presentation of simple food take the place of long hours in the kitchen.

GERMAN RADISH SALAD

Serves 6 to 8

¼ cup vinegar
3 tablespoons olive oil
2 teaspoons salt
½ teaspoon freshly ground pepper
1 pound radishes, sliced (mixed red and white radishes if possible)
1 tablespoon minced fresh parsley

Combine vinegar, oil, salt and pepper, let stand at least 2 hours in a 4-cup Small Wonderlier. Toss with radishes about ½ hour before serving. Serve sprinkled with parsley.

PARTIES

After you've tasted typically German food on home ground, you'll be anxious to add this country's favorite recipes to your cooking repertoire. Invite the heartiest eaters you know to sample Sauerbraten, Bavarian Potato Dumplings, and Bavarian Cream. In addition to this type of hearty food, you'll find the Germans addicted to continental cuisine. One of the world's most elegant fish dinners: Fillet of Sole Werner.

BAVARIAN POTATO DUMPLINGS

18 dumplings

1 pound potatoes
1½ cups flour
1 cup hot milk
1 teaspoon salt
1 large roll, broken in small pieces
2 tablespoons butter

Cook potatoes, peel and put through a fine sieve. Combine with flour, milk and salt. Sauté pieces of roll in butter, set aside. Shape dumplings by hand about the size of a ping pong ball, putting a few pieces of roll in center of each dumpling. Drop in boiling salted water and boil 10 minutes after they rise to surface. If desired, dumplings may be placed on cookie sheet before cooking and frozen. When hard they can be stored in a 2-quart

Wonderlier. When ready to use, thaw dumplings at room temperature, then cook as above.

SAUERBRATEN
FRANKFURT INTER CONTINENTAL

Serves 10 to 12

1 quart vinegar
2 carrots, sliced
2 onions, sliced
12 juniper berries
6 cloves
2 bay leaves
1 tablespoon salt
1 teaspoon pepper
5-pound bottom round or rump roast
¼ cup oil
1 carrot, minced
1 onion, chopped
1 stalk celery, chopped
1 bay leaf
⅛ teaspoon thyme
2 tablespoons tomato paste
3 cups beef bouillon
¼ cup red wine
2 tablespoons sugar
2 tablespoons soy sauce
½ cup flour

Combine vinegar, sliced carrots, sliced onions, juniper berries, cloves, bay leaves, salt and pepper in Roast Flavor Saver. Add meat, cover and store in refrigerator 4 or 5 days. Remove from refrigerator and dry thoroughly. Heat oil in large casserole. Add meat, and brown well on all sides; remove from casserole. Add minced carrot, chopped onion and celery, bay leaf and thyme to casserole. Sauté until vegetables are soft. Add tomato paste and stir until well blended with vegetables. Add bouillon, wine, 1 cup of strained marinade, sugar, soy sauce and meat. Cover and bake in 350°F. oven about 2 hours or until meat is tender. Remove meat from casserole and keep warm. Skim fat from gravy. Thicken with flour and serve over sliced meat.

FILLET OF SOLE WERNER

Serves 4

⅓ cup butter
1 8-ounce box artichoke hearts
½ pound mushrooms, sliced
1½ pounds fillet of sole, cut in strips
4 tomatoes, peeled, cored and minced
¾ cup white wine
1 cup fish stock or clam juice
1 tablespoon butter
1 tablespoon flour
¾ cup hollandaise
⅓ cup heavy cream, whipped
1 tablespoon lemon juice
4 patty shells
4 truffles

Melt butter in large skillet. Add artichokes and sauté 5 minutes. Add mushrooms and sauté another 2 minutes. Add fish and tomatoes. Pour in wine and fish stock and simmer 8 to 10 minutes or until fish flakes. Remove fish and vegetables from skillet and reduce liquid to ⅓ cup. Combine butter and flour and stir into sauce. Cook over low heat until mixture thickens, about 2 minutes. Remove from heat and fold in hollandaise and heavy cream. Add lemon juice and taste; correct seasoning. Add fish and vegetables to sauce and return to heat. Cook just until heated through; do not boil. Spoon into shells, garnish with truffles, serve at once.

BAVARIAN CREAM

Serves 8

6 egg yolks
⅔ cup sugar
1 cup milk
½-inch piece vanilla bean
1½ tablespoons (1½ envelopes) gelatin
¼ cup cold water
4 egg whites
1 tablespoon sugar
1 cup whipped cream
2 tablespoons kirsch

Beat egg yolks until pale and thick. Add sugar gradually, beating well between additions. Boil milk with vanilla bean; gradually add to beaten yolk mixture, beating constantly. Return custard to saucepan and set over moderate heat. Cook, stirring constantly, until mixture thickens and will coat a spoon; remove from heat. Remove vanilla bean. Soften gelatin in cold water, stir into hot custard. Stir until gelatin is dissolved. Chill until thick but not set. Beat egg whites until foamy, add sugar and continue beating until mixture is stiff but not dry. Fold into cooled custard. Fold in whipped cream and kirsch. Spoon into Jel-N-Serve. Cover and refrigerate at least 4 hours before serving.

A typical Bavarian recipe, creamy texture, mild kirsch flavor. Unmolds very well, and will store in refrigerator 2 or 3 days. This may be garnished with raspberries for color.

SNACKS

"Come for coffee and dessert" is one of the easiest ways for a hostess to entertain. The hour, anytime between 11 a.m. and 11 p.m., after that weekly bridge game. Take a cue from Frankfurt – serve desserts in individual portions for anytime coffee snacking. Our fruit desserts can be made ahead and frozen, so you'll always be ready for drop-in company. You can also use these to simplify serving at a large buffet.

PEAR DESSERT

Serves 6

4 egg whites
½ teaspoon cream of tartar
1⅓ cups sugar
2 egg yolks
¾ cup soft, unsalted butter
⅔ cup sifted confectioners sugar
2 teaspoons almond extract
6 stewed pear halves
Caramel Cream (see below)
Whole strawberries

Combine egg whites and cream of tartar in large bowl, beat until foamy. Gradually beat in the 1⅓ cups sugar, a little at a time. Beat until very stiff and glossy. Spread heavy brown paper on a large baking sheet. Mark out 12 circles 2 inches in diameter. Using ½ cup meringue mix per shell, form 6 shells on half the marked circles. Using remaining circles as a guide, form 6 wreaths. Bake in 275°F. oven 1 hour. Turn oven off and leave meringues in to cool. Combine butter, confectioners sugar and almond extract; beat 5 minutes or until buttercream is fluffy. Place in a 2-cup Wonderlier and refrigerate until ready to use. When meringues are completely cooled remove from oven and gently take off brown paper. Spread buttercream on the bottom and rims of the 6 meringue shells. Place the meringue wreaths on top of the bottom shells in layer cake fashion. Place assembled shells on cookie sheet and freeze until firm. Remove from cookie sheet and place in Pie Taker, freeze until ready to serve. To serve, place a stewed pear half, cut side down, on top of each meringue. Cover with caramel cream and garnish with whole strawberries. Meringues should be removed from freezer at least 15 minutes before serving.

CARAMEL CREAM

3½ cups sauce

4 egg yolks
1 cup brown sugar
⅓ cup sifted flour
2 cups hot milk
1 tablespoon butter
1 tablespoon vanilla extract

Beat yolks until thick and lemon colored, gradually beat in sugar until well blended. Add flour and mix thoroughly. Gradually add milk, beating constantly. Place caramel cream over moderate heat, cook to boiling, beating constantly. Let boil 1 to 2 minutes, being careful that mixture does not burn. Remove from heat and beat in butter and vanilla. Pour into 4-cup Wonderlier and freeze or refrigerate until ready to use.

PLUM PIE

Serves 6

2 cups sliced fresh or frozen plums
sugar
cinnamon
1 tablespoon quick tapioca
1 cup biscuit mix
⅓ cup cream
1 tablespoon sugar
1 tablespoon chopped almonds
Hot Custard Sauce (recipe below)

Spread fruit on bottom of individual ½-cup ramekins. Sprinkle with sugar and cinnamon. Sprinkle each with ½ teaspoon tapioca. Combine biscuit mix, cream, sugar and nuts, mix with a fork to soften dough. Beat vigorously about 20 strokes. Knead lightly on floured board and roll dough ½-inch thick. Cut into six 3-inch circles. Place on top of ramekins, pressing down on edges to seal. Prick tops to allow steam to escape. Bake in 425°F. oven 20 to 25 minutes, or until fruit is tender and top is brown. Serve with hot custard sauce.

HOT CUSTARD SAUCE

about 1 cup

1 cup sugar
⅓ cup water
2 egg yolks
⅛ teaspoon salt
2 tablespoons cognac

Combine sugar and water in saucepan. Cook over moderate heat, stirring constantly, until sugar is dissolved. Beat yolks with salt and gradually add syrup, beating constantly. Cook over moderate heat until thickened. Add cognac, stir well.

Geneva

Switzerland is a picture-postcard country. Its towering mountains, the grandeur of its lakes, its quaint villages—all are incredibly beautiful. Get your fill of the magnificent countryside by hiring a car, heading for the mountains. Fun, too, is a walking tour through one of the many interesting cities. In Geneva, visit la Vielle Ville, the old city. Walk through its cobblestone streets, take time to visit the beautiful old cathedral, and be tempted by the wares of the many antique shops.

PICNICS

The Swiss picnic on raw ham and Bindenfleisch. The latter is dried meat of mountain cattle, steeped in red wine, dried in the open air. Sliced paper thin, it is served with bread, pickles, and small white onions. Gruyere, emmenthaler and tilsit make good picnic cheeses. Raclette, a variation on fondue, can be eaten in a restaurant or picnic-style before an open fire.

RACLETTE

Serves 15 to 20

½ wheel Bagnes cheese
new potatoes, cooked in their jackets and peeled
pickled onions
sour gherkins

Place the cut portion of the cheese against the heat of a Raclette grill. (The cheese may be heated before any upright hot grill, whether charcoal, gas or electric.) Turn 2 or 3 times to prevent the melted cheese from dripping, if possible. When the cheese is at the bubbling stage, scrape it with a knife onto a hot plate. This is one serving. Repeat until the guests have had sufficient servings. When the cheese is served, pass a bowl of hot potatoes and trays of pickled onions and sour gherkins.

PARTIES

Any well-balanced file of party recipes should include the following categories: The Big Splurge—elegant, expensive luxury entrée that looks it; The Unexpected—a new way with an old favorite; The Quickie — a main dish that takes less than half an hour to cook, but looks and tastes as if you'd slaved over it. In one fell swoop, recipes to fit all three requirements: Filet of Beef Wellington, Roast Beef in Crust, and Minced Veal.

MINCED VEAL GENEVA INTER CONTINENTAL

Serves 4

2 pounds veal steak, cut ½ inch thick
1 teaspoon salt
¼ teaspoon pepper
3 tablespoons butter
¼ cup dry white wine
1½ cups heavy cream
2 tablespoons brandy

Swiss picnics happen everywhere in the beautiful countryside.

Cut veal into large julienne strips, dry thoroughly, season well. Place 2 tablespoons butter in large skillet over moderately high heat. When foam starts to subside, add veal. Sauté about 8 minutes, browning well on all sides. Remove meat and keep warm. Add wine to skillet and cook until liquid has reduced to about ¼ cup. Add cream, simmer 5 minutes until cream has reduced and thickened slightly. Taste, correct seasoning. Add meat, remaining butter and brandy. Mix well; let simmer 1 minute or until meat is heated thoroughly. Serve at once.

A rich, creamy, delicately flavored veal dish. Very good, very French in feeling.

The makings for Raclette: fine Bagnes cheese to be melted, scraped, and then combined with onions, potatoes, gherkins.

ROAST BEEF IN CRUST

Serves 8 to 10

1 4-pound rolled rib roast
1½ packages pie crust mix
6 tablespoons milk
1 egg, slightly beaten

Place roast in a shallow pan flat side up. Season with salt and pepper. Insert meat thermometer in center of meat. Roast in 300°F. oven, allowing 30 minutes per pound for rare, or about 2 hours. Add about 15 minutes for medium and 30 minutes for well done, using markings on thermometer to check degree of doneness. Remove from oven and cool enough to handle. Prepare pastry according to package directions, using milk in place of water. Roll to ⅛-inch thickness, fit around roast. Sprinkle edges with water and press to seal. Place on flat baking sheet, seam side down. Brush with beaten egg. Decorate top of pastry with remaining pieces of pastry if desired. Bake in 425°F. oven 20 to 25 minutes or until pastry is golden and flaky.

There is good contrast in textures here, and the crust makes the roast very attractive.

BEEF WELLINGTON

Serves 8

1 4-pound filet of beef
salt
pepper
3 strips bacon
½ cup coarsely chopped celery
1 small onion, sliced
1 bay leaf, crumbled

¼ teaspoon dried rosemary
4 cups flour
1 teaspoon salt
¼ pound (1 stick) butter
½ cup shortening
2 eggs
8 ounces pâté de foie gras
½ cup ice water
1 cup veal stock

Trim filet, sprinkle with salt and pepper, cover with bacon strips. Place in a shallow baking pan with vegetables and rosemary. Roast in a 450°F. oven 15 minutes for rare, 20 to 25 minutes for medium. Remove from oven. Remove bacon, cool to room temperature. Combine flour and salt, cut in shortening until mixture is like coarse meal. Add 1 egg and enough ice water to make a dough. Chill in a Square Round. When filet is cool, spread with all but ¼ cup of the pâté. Roll out pastry to ⅛-inch thickness. Place filet on pastry, trim edges so pastry covers meat. Moisten edges with a little cold water and press firmly together. Brush the pastry with remaining egg, lightly beaten. Place filet, on baking sheet, seam side down, and bake in 450°F. oven for 15 to 20 minutes, or until the pastry is nicely browned. Heat the veal stock and add the remaining ¼ cup pâté; simmer 15 minutes, stirring from time to time to keep sauce smooth. Serve with the filet.

SNACKS

Not all recipes can be considered Party, Picnic and *Snack fare, but Swiss Onion Pie can. Eat this tasty, light quiche as a snack in one of the many tiny, charming Swiss ski villages. St. Cergue is just a one-hour drive past Lake Geneva and up through the mountains. The recipe we brought home will enable you to enjoy this Swiss specialty at a summer luncheon—or why not carry it with you to add zest to your first spring picnic?*

ONION PIE

Serves 6 to 8

½ pound onions thinly sliced (about 2 cups)
2 tablespoons butter
8 eggs
1 cup dry white wine
⅔ cup heavy cream
1 teaspoon salt
⅛ teaspoon pepper
⅛ teaspoon grated nutmeg
½ pound grated Gruyere cheese (about 2 cups)
1 9-inch pie crust

Sauté onions in butter until soft, remove from heat and set aside. Combine eggs, wine, cream, salt, pepper and nutmeg. Spread one cup of grated cheese on bottom of pastry shell, cover with onions and top with remaining cheese. Pour cream mixture over cheese and onions. Bake in 350°F. oven 1 hour or until top of pie is brown and a knife inserted in center of custard comes out clean. Remove from oven, place in Pie Taker and chill.

A very tasty, light quiche with a beautiful appearance and creamy texture.

LONDON

London has a new image. It's no longer just the city where history has been made. London is the now *city of Europe, where things are happening. It all started with the change of pace from classic tweeds to Carnaby Street mod; now Britain sets a fast clip in many fields, waiting for the rest of the world to catch up. Enjoy this new tempo in London as a bonus; it's still the time-honored tradition and the familiar landmarks of this majestic city that will delight the average tourist.*

PICNICS

Off to Ascot for the races, taking a train to visit one of the stately country homes of Britain, or leaving by car for a trip to the continent, picnic gloriously as the British do on such exquisite food as handsome Galantine of Duck, Game Pie or roast stuffed chicken. All of these dishes can be bought in London, consumed on your boat trip anywhere that the Thames beckons.

GALANTINE OF DUCK

8 to 10 servings

1 4 to 5 pound duckling
¼ cup cognac
¾ pound boneless veal, ground
¾ pound boneless lean pork, ground
4 ounces pâté foie gras
2 tablespoons butter
2 shallots, chopped
½ cup chopped onion
1 tablespoon chopped parsley
1½ teaspoons salt
¼ teaspoon tarragon

Elegant picnic dish: Galantine of Duck.

¼ teaspoon thyme
1 cup heavy cream
¼ cup chopped pistachio nuts
2 truffles, chopped (optional)
½ cup sliced onion
½ cup sliced celery
1 carrot, sliced
1 sprig parsley
4 cups rich duck stock made from bones of duck
Chaud-Froid Blanc (recipe below)
black and green olives
Clear Aspic (recipe below)

Bone the duckling or have it boned. Using a sharp knife remove all the meat from the skin, leaving a shell. Discard any excess fat removed from duck. Cut meat from the drumsticks and breast into ⅓-inch cubes; marinate in cognac for 2 hours. Grind remaining duck meat and combine with other ground meats and pâté. Melt butter in small skillet, add shallot and onion. Sauté until onion is soft. Add to ground meat mixture along with parsley, salt, tarragon and thyme. Drain cognac and add to ground meat mixture along with cream. Beat to make a smooth paste. Lay duck, skin side outside, on a flat surface and spread with ground meat mixture. Over this lay marinated duck meat. Sprinkle with pistachio nuts and truffles. Shape into firm roll, drawing edges together along length of the roll and at ends. Carefully sew the edges of the skin. Place roll on a large, well-buttered piece of clean linen. Roll tightly and tie at both ends and in the middle. The roll should be smooth and even. Place the vegetables in a large kettle and put galantine on top. Cover with stock. Bring to a boil and simmer gently 1½ hours. Cool in stock, remove, unroll and roll again in clean cloth. Place in Jumbo Bread Server, weight and let stand 2 hours. Cover with Chaud-Froid Blanc, olives, aspic, as described below. When set, galantine may be replaced in Bread Server and held a day or two before serving.

CHAUD-FROID BLANC

2 tablespoons gelatin
2 tablespoons water
1 cup mayonnaise

Combine gelatin and water. Stir over hot water until gelatin is dissolved. Beat into mayonnaise, cool until thickened but not set.

CLEAR ASPIC

1 tablespoon gelatin
2 cups clear duck stock

Soften gelatin in ½ cup cold stock. Blend in remaining stock and stir over low heat until gelatin has dissolved. Chill until thickened.

To decorate: Remove cloth, then remove stitching from well-chilled galantine. Place on a wire rack in a roasting pan. Spoon a little Chaud-Froid over galantine, chill briefly. Repeat until galantine is completely covered with Chaud-Froid Blanc. Decorate with sliced olives to form an attractive pattern. Cover the galantine with the clear aspic, using the same technique as for the Chaud-Froid. Keep the galantine chilled until ready to serve.

SUMMER PUDDING

Serves 4

5 to 6 slices white bread
1 pound fresh fruit (raspberries and red currants if available)
½ cup sugar
½ cup water
⅛ teaspoon cinnamon

Trim crusts from bread and line a 3-cup Wonderlier with bread, cutting the slices to fit together tightly. Combine fruit, sugar, water and cinnamon in small saucepan. Cook over low heat until the fruit is just soft, about 6 to 8 minutes. Fill the center of the lined bowl with the hot fruit. Cover the top with another slice of bread, press it down and pour more juice over it. Place a small weight on top of the bread so that it presses down on the fruit. Chill well. Turn out of bowl onto a dish or serve from bowl. Serve with whipped cream.

Delicious juice soaks into bread to make a soft bread pudding-type dessert. It unmolds well.

GAME PIE

Serves 6 to 8

½ pound sliced bacon, partially cooked
2 3-pound pheasants, boned and quartered
1 large onion, finely chopped
½ pound mushrooms, sliced
½ cup well-seasoned pheasant stock (made from bird bones)
¼ cup Madeira
2 tablespoons flour
Pastry (recipe below)

Line a 4-quart casserole with well-drained bacon. If domestic, fatty pheasants are used, trim away all excess fat from bird before cooking. If wild young birds are used this will not be necessary. Place pheasant quarters on top of bacon. Top with onion, mushrooms and stock. Blend Madeira with flour to make paste, pour into casserole. Cover with pastry, cut several slits for steam to escape, and bake in 350°F. oven 1½ hours for the domestic birds, 2 hours for wild pheasants.

PASTRY

1 cup flour
¼ teaspoon salt
1 tablespoon shortening
1 small egg
3 tablespoons milk
¼ cup butter

Sift flour and salt, add shortening and cut in with a fork until mixture is well blended. Combine egg and milk and add to dry ingredients. Mix well. On floured Pastry Sheet, roll dough to 1/6-inch thickness. Cut butter into small pieces and arrange over center third of pastry. Fold unbuttered portions of pastry over center. Press around edges to seal and roll out to original shape. Repeat this folding and rolling process two more times. Roll to shape of casserole.

PARTIES

Tea for two savored in the cozy warmth of a lovely home or in elegant surroundings can be one of your pleasantest memories of England. To help you prepare an

Tea in England: Dundee Cake, Clotted Cream, Biscuits—and, of course, a pot of hot tea, and a magnificent view.

authentic English tea in your own home, we've brought back recipes typical of what is served. "Cream teas" are a special custom and best known in Devon. Devonshire clotted cream – you can substitute whipped cream – is heaped on buttered scones spread with strawberry jam.

DEVONSHIRE CLOTTED CREAM

6½ cups cream

2 quarts half-and-half

Pour half-and-half into a broad flat earthenware or enamel pan and let stand 24 hours. Set it on low heat and heat slowly to scald, never boil. When the cream cracks across the center remove it from the heat. Let it stand in a cool place overnight before skimming off the cream. Remaining ½ cup liquid can be used in puddings, sauces or custard.

DUNDEE CAKE

1 8-inch square cake

¾ cup butter
⅔ cup sugar
3 eggs
2 cups sifted flour
1 teaspoon baking powder
½ teaspoon salt
1 cup currants
¾ cup chopped dates
¾ cup raisins
½ cup mixed chopped peel
3 tablespoons split blanched almonds

Cream butter and sugar until light and fluffy. Add eggs, one at a time, beating well after each addition. Reserve 2 tablespoons flour; sift remaining flour with baking powder and salt. Add

flour, baking powder mixture to butter, blending thoroughly. Mix the reserved flour with the fruits until they are well coated. Stir in fruit and mixed peel. Spoon into greased 8-inch square cake pan. Bake in 350°F. oven 30 minutes. Arrange almonds attractively on top. Turn oven to 325°F. for 30 minutes, or until cake tests done.

A light, not too fruity, fruit-type cake. Really very tasty and attractive. Freezes well in Snack-Stor.

SNACKS

London is one city where you can spend weeks taking daily excursions to interesting towns. Travel in any direction: north to the cathedral of St. Albans; southwest to Kew Gardens; southeast to Canterbury; or west to Stratford-on-Avon. Stop at a picturesque pub for Veal, Ham and Egg Pie — most typical British snack. Serve this tasty dish for your at-home snacking as it would be in London—with brown onions, pickles and tomatoes.

VEAL, HAM AND EGG PIE

Serves 4 to 6

1½ cups flour
½ teaspoon salt
½ cup (1 stick) butter
5 tablespoons water
1½ pounds stewing veal, cut in small pieces
¼ pound cooked ham, cut in small pieces
½ teaspoon salt
¼ teaspoon thyme leaves
1 teaspoon grated lemon rind
3 hard-cooked eggs, shelled
1 egg, slightly beaten
1 envelope (1 tablespoon) gelatin
1 cup chicken broth

Sift flour and salt into a bowl. Heat butter and water together until butter melts, then bring rapidly to a boil. Pour into flour and mix well until cool enough to handle. Continue mixing and kneading until the dough is smooth. Shape dough into a ball, cover and let rest in warm place for ½ hour. Roll out to ½-inch thickness, reserving about 1/6th for the top. Grease a 9 x 5 x 3-inch loaf pan and line with pastry, carefully molding it onto the bottom and sides and making sure there are no air pockets. Combine meat, seasoning, lemon rind. Pack half the mixture tightly into the pastry. Arrange the hard-cooked eggs down the center. Pack in remaining mixture, filling tightly. Roll out the top pastry to about ½-inch thickness. Dampen edges of both top and pie. Cover filling with top and press edges together. Trim the edges and pinch in a decorative fashion. Make a hole in the center of the top and decorate around it with pastry leaves made from leftover pastry scraps. Brush with beaten egg. Bake in 350°F. oven 1½ hours. Meanwhile, sprinkle gelatin over chicken broth in small saucepan; let stand to soften. Heat, stirring constantly, until gelatin is dissolved. Let pie cool on wire rack 30 minutes. Then slowly pour broth mixture, through a small funnel, into center of pie. Let cool 2 hours longer; refrigerate in Bread Server overnight.

Most people either love Paris or hate it. Few quarrel about the quality of the food. The French are undoubtedly the most inventive of cooks, and whether you dine in one of the restaurants renowned for its haute cuisine or in some tiny place you discover by accident or recommendation, you'll eat superbly. In Paris, we set out to find recipes not overly familiar to American palates. Onion Soup is the exception. Once you've eaten it at Les Halles you'll want to duplicate it at home.

PICNICS

A small restaurant in St. Germain-des-Prés gave us our Paris picnic. As you sit down, you're served an aperitif of white wine and framboise in a minute crock. Then a cart is wheeled in topped with three layers of larger crocks filled with pâtés and salads. You can easily duplicate this lavish idea for picnicking if you carry the food in appropriate Tupperware containers.

PICKLED MUSHROOMS

Serves 8

1 large onion, minced
1 clove garlic, minced
2 cups dry white wine
½ cup cider vinegar
2 bay leaves
½ teaspoon dried thyme
½ teaspoon freshly ground pepper
½ teaspoon salt
½ cup olive oil

Above: Les Halles—its onion soup means Paris to many a traveler.

1½ pounds button mushrooms
⅓ cup sour cream
2 tablespoons heavy cream
chopped chives

Combine onion, garlic, wine, vinegar, bay leaves, thyme, pepper and salt in saucepan. Bring to boil and simmer 5 minutes. Add oil. Remove stems from mushrooms and add to pan; simmer until mushrooms are tender, about 10 minutes. Pour into 2-quart Wonderlier and chill thoroughly. Before serving, combine sour cream and heavy cream, drain mushrooms and blend with sour cream mixture. Sprinkle with chives. Serve very cold.

TURKISH ONIONS

Serves 4 to 6

¼ cup olive oil
1 pound small white onions, peeled
1 pound can (about 2 cups) stewed tomatoes
⅓ cup white raisins
1½ teaspoons salt
½ teaspoon fresh ground pepper
¼ teaspoon oregano

Heat oil in saucepan, add onions and sauté 5 minutes, stirring occasionally. Combine remaining ingredients, bring to a boil, cover and simmer 1 hour, removing the cover for the last 10 minutes. Pour into a 1-quart Wonderlier and chill thoroughly.

EGGS IN GELATIN

Serves 6

2 cups chicken broth
1 tablespoon gelatin
6 tablespoons mayonnaise
½ teaspoon salt
6 cold soft-poached eggs
6 tablespoons diced ham (about ¼ pound)
6 slices truffle

Skim all fat from chicken broth. Sprinkle the gelatin into ½ cup broth, stir until softened. Combine with remaining broth and cook over moderate heat, stirring constantly, until gelatin is completely dissolved. Stir in salt and remove from heat. Combine mayonnaise with 3 tablespoons of gelatin mixture and chill until thick but not set. Pour ⅛ inch of gelatin into each of 6 Sauce Dishes; chill 10 minutes or until gelatin is set. Place 1 egg in each dish. Place 1 tablespoon thickened mayonnaise mixture on one side of egg and 1 tablespoon diced ham on other side of egg in each dish. Place truffle on top of egg and carefully spoon almost-set gelatin over all, filling each Sauce Dish to top. Refrigerate until ready to serve, at least one hour.

PARTIES

Our first taste of filet of lamb was in an antique-filled Parisian restaurant, a former convent that dates back to the year 1610. Reportedly, this is where the Dauphin was proclaimed King of France. Of course, it is trite to say that Roast Filet of Lamb Marfeuille is fit to set before a King—but it is that *good. For a fittingly royal finish to your party, bring on a dessert as impressive as the lamb, Quatrefoil French Fruit Tart.*

FRENCH FRUIT TART

1 10-inch tart

PUFF PASTRY

½ pound (2 bars) sweet butter, chilled
2 cups sifted all-purpose flour
1 teaspoon salt
1 cup ice water

Cut each bar of butter in half lengthwise. Place on a sheet of waxed paper, side by side, to form a rectangle. Refrigerate until ready to use. Sift flour and salt into large mixing bowl. Stir in ice water, mixing with fork, until well combined (dough will be dry). Mix dough with hands until there are no traces of dry flour; shape into a ball. On unfloured surface, knead dough until smooth and elastic—5 to 10 minutes. Cover with a towel and let rest 20 minutes. On floured Pastry Sheet roll out dough to 6 x 11-inch rectangle. Place butter strips on half of dough, ½ inch from sides. Fold other half of dough over butter; press edges together firmly with Rolling Pin or fingertips to seal. Refrigerate, wrapped in foil, 30 minutes. With Rolling Pin tap dough lightly several times to flatten butter. On floured Pastry Sheet roll out lengthwise into a 6 x 11-inch rectangle. From short side, fold dough into thirds, making sure edges and corners are even; press edges to seal. Refrigerate, covered, 30 minutes. Place dough on lightly floured surface with folded side of dough at right. Starting from center, with quick, light strokes, roll out dough to a 6 x 11-inch rectangle. Fold in thirds, as above. Refrigerate, covered, 30 minutes. Repeat the rolling, folding and chilling of dough 4 more times. Divide dough in half. Place each half in a Square Round. Refrigerate half to use for tart, freeze other half for use when desired.

French Fruit Tart: glorious results, and easy, if made as a two-day project.

FRUIT TART

Place dough on a floured Pastry Sheet. If the dough is hard, beat it with the Rolling Pin to soften, then knead to a fairly flat circle. It should be just soft enough to roll without cracking. Roll dough into a circle ⅛-inch thick and 12 inches in diameter. Line a cookie sheet with a double thickness of heavy brown paper. Place a 10-inch flan ring on paper. Ease pastry into center of ring to make an even, rounded rim. Press a decorative edge around pastry with fingers. Line with wax paper or foil and fill with uncooked dry white beans or rice. (This weighs dough down, preventing it from puffing or blistering.) Bake in 450°F. oven about 15 minutes or until pastry starts to brown. Remove rice and wax paper; continue baking until bottom is brown and flaky, about 10 minutes more. Cool, remove from flan ring. Store in Pie Taker until ready to fill.

TART FILLING

1 1-pound can bing cherries, drained
pineapple slices, drained
apricots, drained
peaches, drained
¾ cup apricot jelly or jam
1 tablespoon cognac
confectioners sugar

Place all drained fruit on paper towels and dry completely, set aside. Combine jelly and cognac in small saucepan. Cook, stirring constantly over moderate heat, until jelly is completely melted. Paint the bottom of the pastry generously with the hot glaze. Sprinkle the edges of pastry with powdered sugar. Fill with the dried fruits, in any decorative pattern desired. Brush with remaining glaze. If glaze has hardened, return to heat until soft enough to paint fruit easily. Store in Pie Taker until ready to serve. Tart should be served the same day it is filled or the pastry will become soggy from the fruit.

This is a very light flaky dough and a beautiful dessert. If the pastry is done one day and rolled and filled the next, this is not a difficult recipe.

ROAST FILET OF LAMB MARFEUILLE

Serves 3

1 3-pound rack of lamb, boned
(1-pound filet of lamb)
1 dill pickle
3 flat anchovies
¼ cup bread crumbs
1 tablespoon capers, finely chopped
1 tablespoon finely chopped parsley
1 shallot, finely chopped
1 cooked mushroom, finely chopped
1 clove garlic, finely chopped
⅛ teaspoon dried thyme
⅛ teaspoon dried tarragon
⅛ teaspoon dried basil
Wine Sauce (recipe below)

Make a long, deep slit down center of lamb, lengthwise, making sure not to cut all the way through. Cut 3 julienne strips from pickle and lay down center of lamb. Top with anchovies. Roll Filet tightly and tie like a roast to maintain long shape. Roast in 325°F. oven for 30 minutes or until meat thermometer reads 140°F. Combine remaining ingredients and spread over roast. Continue roasting until thermometer reads 145° to 150°F, about 15 minutes. Meat should be rare. Slice roast quite thin, and serve covered with the wine sauce.

WINE SAUCE

1 onion, finely chopped
3 tablespoons butter
1 tablespoon flour
½ cup dry white wine
1 tablespoon lemon juice
2 teaspoons chopped parsley

1 bay leaf
1/8 teaspoon dried thyme

Sauté onion in 2 tablespoons butter until soft but not brown. Add flour and brown slightly. Add remaining ingredients, except remaining tablespoon butter. Simmer over low heat, covered, 15 minutes. Strain sauce and whip in the remaining tablespoon of butter.

This is a most elegant dish. Not only is the cut of meat one of the finest available but the sauce is perfectly beautiful!

SNACKS

Les Halles, as everyone knows, is the place to go for France's most famous snack, Onion Soup. If you can get to Paris before the end of 1968, when the market moves to the suburbs, you'll be able to savor all the color, smells and excitement of this aging French landmark. In a daintier mood, visit Fauchon's—there's no food emporium like it anywhere.

ONION SOUP

Serves 6

6 large onions, thinly sliced
1/4 pound (1 stick) butter
1 tablespoon salt
1 teaspoon Dijon mustard
1/8 teaspoon pepper
1/8 teaspoon dried thyme
4 cups chicken broth
1/3 cup dry white wine
6 teaspoons calvados
6 slices French bread
grated Parmesan cheese

Sauté onions in butter until tender. Add salt, mustard, pepper and thyme and stir until mustard is well blended. Add chicken broth and wine and bring to a boil. Ladle into 6 heatproof soup dishes; put 1 teaspoon calvados in each serving. Top with French bread and sprinkle liberally with grated cheese. Place under broiler briefly, until cheese is brown. Serve at once.

ROQUEFORT SANDWICHES

4 sandwiches or 16 tea sandwiches

Blend 1/4 pound Roquefort cheese with 1/4 pound butter and 1 tablespoon armagnac. Spread 3 tablespoons of mixture on a slice of bread, top with another slice and trim crusts. Repeat to make three more sandwiches. For tea sandwiches cut each large sandwich in quarters.

NUT AND PATE SANDWICHES

4 sandwiches or 16 tea sandwiches

Blend 1/4 cup ground almonds, 1/4 cup butter and 1/4 cup pâté de foie gras until smooth. Spread 3 tablespoons of mixture on a slice of bread, top with another slice and trim crusts. Repeat to make three more sandwiches. For tea sandwiches cut each large sandwich in quarters.

Both are delicious, lovely with a salad and tea. Can be frozen in Cold Cut Keeper.

ROME

Rome is a city of many impressions. Fall under its captivating spell and you'll see ghosts of Caesars stalking the streets. You'll find that the 20th century Romans have an irrepressible gusto all their own. You can't escape Via Veneto—besides, hours spent in its lively sidewalk cafés with those endless cups of cappuccino let you enjoy Rome effortlessly. Try fettucine by all means, but who's to say you'll pick the right Alfredo's? And don't limit yourself to pasta—try everything.

PICNICS

Picnic in style, effortlessly, by visiting a rosticceria or salumeria, buzzing places that specialize in take-out dishes. What's delightful is the unfamiliar food —you can avoid the routine ham and cheese. Sample finocchi and carrot salad, a sandwich on tomato bread. Cold dishes go picnicking to Adrian's Villa; serve hot dishes to make a feast of an at-home picnic.

SPINACH PIE

Serves 6 to 8

Crust for 9-inch pie
2 10-ounce packages frozen chopped spinach
2 eggs, slightly beaten
⅓ cup grated Parmesan cheese

Bake crust in 425°F. oven 5 minutes, cool. Cook spinach according to package directions, drain well. Add eggs and cheese, blend well. Spread evenly in pie shell. Bake in 425°F. oven for 10 minutes. Lower heat to 350°F. and bake another 20 minutes, or until pie is set. Cool, store in Pie Taker until ready to use.

Unusual way to serve a vegetable. The pie is much tastier cold than hot. Serve with baked ham or chicken in wine.

LATTICE-TOP PIE CRUST

Pastry for 2-crust pie

Line pan with half of pastry, trim leaving 1-inch overhanging edge. Fill. Roll rest of pastry; cut into ½-inch strips, using Pastry Pal. Moisten edge of bottom pastry with water. Lay half of pastry strips across filling 1 inch apart. Weave first cross strip through center. Add another cross strip and weave, placing across top of lattice where first strip went under and under where first strip went on top. Continue weaving until lattice is complete. Fold lower crust over pastry strips. Press firmly around edge to seal. Bake in hot 425°F. oven for 10 minutes. Lower heat to moderate 350°F. and bake another 20 minutes or until pie is set.

Making the lattice is no trouble once you get the hang of it. The rich green filling looks very appetizing through the top.

CALZONI

Serves 4

1¼ cups lukewarm water
¼ teaspoon salt
1 package of cake yeast
3 tablespoons oil
4 cups flour
¼ pound mozzarella, thinly sliced

The Piazza Navona—and Chocolate Tartufo.

¼ pound prosciutto
¼ pound salami
¼ teaspoon ground pepper
⅛ teaspoon salt

Measure ¼ cup water into small bowl. Sprinkle or crumble yeast into water; stir until yeast is dissolved. Pour 1 cup water into large bowl, add salt and 2 tablespoons oil. Stir in 3 cups flour, beat thoroughly. Gradually add remaining flour until dough handles easily. Turn out onto floured Pastry Sheet, knead until smooth, about two or three minutes. Divide dough in half. Roll half to 10-inch diameter. Brush with remaining tablespoon oil, leaving outside edge dry. Sprinkle remaining ingredients over circle, top with other half of dough rolled out to a 10-inch circle. Brush bottom edge of calzoni with water and pinch edges to seal tightly. Place on greased cookie sheet. Bake in 425°F. oven 30 minutes. Cool and place in Pie Taker to store.

PARTIES

Put some pep in pasta! Start by choosing several of the most unusual shapes and sizes. Vary the pasta sauces also; we'd serve four. If you're feeling really magnanimous you might want to add a great lasagna dish. That's your Pasta Party — a do-ahead job with your freezer your ally. Even your salads—do have more than one type (Tomato and Mushroom, Endive and Watercress)—can be made ahead; store and serve in Fix-N-Mix bowls.

LASAGNA IMBOTTITE

Serves 8

1 pound lasagna noodles
6 cups Neapolitan Sauce
1 pound ricotta cheese
1 egg
1 pound mozzarella cheese, thinly sliced
1 cup diced ham (½ pound)
Meatballs (recipe below)
½ cup grated Parmesan cheese

Cook noodles according to package directions, drain. Spread a thin layer of sauce on the bottom of a 15 x 9 x 2-inch casserole Place ⅓ of noodles on bottom. Mix ricotta and egg, spread half over noodles in casserole. Cover with half of the mozzarella and all of the ham. Add a second layer of noodles and cover with remaining ricotta, mozzarella and all of meatballs. Pour over ½ of sauce. Add remaining noodles and top with remaining sauce. Sprinkle with Parmesan cheese. Cover and bake in 350°F. oven for 1½ hours.

MEATBALLS

1 slice white bread
½ cup water
½ pound ground beef
2 tablespoons Parmesan cheese
1 teaspoon parsley flakes
1 teaspoon salt
½ teaspoon grated lemon peel
½ teaspoon ground fennel seed
⅛ teaspoon grated nutmeg
⅛ teaspoon ground pepper
1 egg, slightly beaten
1 clove garlic, crushed
2 tablespoons oil

Soak bread in water, squeeze dry. Combine with all ingredients except oil. Moisten hands and form into balls about the size of ping pong balls. Heat oil in large frypan. Add meatballs and brown well on all sides.

NEAPOLITAN SAUCE

4 cups

2 tablespoons olive oil
1 teaspoon bacon fat
1 onion, chopped
1 carrot, chopped
½ cup chopped celery
4 tomatoes, peeled, seeded, chopped
½ cup water
2 tablespoons tomato paste
1 clove garlic, crushed
1½ teaspoon dried basil or 2 tablespoons fresh basil
1½ teaspoon salt
dash pepper

Heat oil and bacon fat in large saucepan. Add onion, carrot, celery; sauté until brown. Add remaining ingredients and simmer 1½ hours.

This is a thinner sauce than others, with a fine tomato flavor.

BOLOGNESE SAUCE

2 cups

2 tablespoons olive oil
½ cup chopped parsley

Overlooking the Spanish Steps: Spinach Pie.

½ cup chopped onion
½ cup chopped celery
2 carrots, chopped
¼ pound ground beef
2 ounces Italian sweet sausage
½ cup tomato sauce
½ teaspoon salt
dash pepper
½ ounce dry mushrooms, reconstituted
⅓ cup chianti wine

Heat oil in large saucepan. Add vegetables and sauté until onion is soft. Add meat and cook until brown. Add tomato sauce, salt and pepper. Simmer gently, covered, about half an hour; add mushrooms and wine and cook another half hour or until sauce is thick.

This is excellent sauce, almost like a stew Italian style. Served over pasta it makes a complete main dish.

MUSHROOM SAUCE

2 cups

1 carrot, chopped
½ medium onion, chopped
¼ cup chopped celery
4 slices bacon, cooked and drained
½ ounce dried mushrooms, reconstituted
½ cup hot water
3 tablespoons Bolognese Sauce
1 tablespoon tomato sauce
½ teaspoon salt
¼ teaspoon oregano

Combine all ingredients in a large saucepan. Simmer 45 minutes, until sauce is quite thick.

This is more of a stew-like sauce, this time with a smoky bacon flavor. Very good, very different — would serve too as a main dish over noodles.

PESTO GENOVESE

About ¾ cup sauce

12 large, fresh basil leaves
6 cloves garlic, minced
⅓ cup grated Parmesan cheese
⅓ cup pine nuts
2 tablespoons chopped parsley
½ teaspoon salt
½ cup olive oil

Crush and blend basil, garlic, cheese, nuts, parsley and salt in blender or with a mortar and pestle until mixture is a smooth paste. Still blending, gradually add the oil; mix thoroughly until smooth. To serve, spoon over hot pasta, toss quickly and lightly, add more Parmesan.

This is really a green herb sauce, very garlicky but wonderfully so. This must be made with fresh basil to achieve the true basil flavor and lovely color.

SNACKS

The Romans love ice cream in unusual fruit flavors like fig, grape and apricot. In the Piazza Navona, often called the most beautiful square in the world, linger at a sidewalk cafe facing the 17th century Bernini fountains and gorge yourself on luscious Chocolate Tartufo, an ice cream dessert as beautiful as it is delicious. Or snack on Mozzarella in Carroza. Or try Suppli di Risso — rice-ham balls with a melting center surprise.

Rome, a city of fountains — wonderful background for wonderful Italian food.

CHOCOLATE TARTUFO TRE SCALINI

15 Servings

1 quart milk
6 envelopes no-melt unsweetened chocolate
5 egg yolks
2 cups sugar
30 candied cherries
12 ounces sweet chocolate, finely chopped

Combine milk and chocolate in a saucepan. Cook over low heat, stirring constantly, until chocolate is completely melted. Beat egg yolks until thick and lemon colored; beat in sugar. Beat in hot chocolate mixture a little at a time, beating constantly until well blended. Cook over low heat, stirring constantly, for 2 minutes. Remove from heat and pour into a 2-quart Wonderlier. Freeze until mixture is thick

enough to handle. Form 30 balls with candied cherries inside, using about 3 tablespoons mixture per ball. Roll in chopped chocolate and place in Pie Taker. Return to freezer until ready to serve. Remove from freezer 10 minutes before serving. Serve covered with whipped cream. Hint: Form 3 or 4 balls at a time, then, return balls and mixture to freezer, wait about 10 minutes, or until mixture again is hard enough to work with.

These are really hard to resist—the combination of textures of the crunchy coating, creamy inside and whipped cream outside is fantastic.

MOZZARELLA IN CARROZA

Serves 4 to 6

8 slices white bread
8 thin slices mozzarella cheese
4 slices ham, or ½ cup sliced, cooked mushrooms, or 12 flat anchovies
2 eggs
¼ cup milk
oil

Remove crusts from bread. Flour cheese lightly and place 1 slice each on 4 slices of bread. Cover with the ham or the mushroom slices or the anchovies. Top with remaining slices of bread. (May be stored in Cold Cut Keeper at this point and finished off just before serving.) Beat eggs with milk, dip sandwiches in this mixture. Pour oil in a large skillet to depth of 1 inch. Heat until hot but not smoking, about 360°F. Fry sandwiches on one side until bread is golden. Turn and top each with remaining slices of cheese. Cover skillet and cook until bread is golden and cheese melted. Serve at once.

SUPPLI DI RISO

32 rice balls

4 cups boiling water
4 tablespoons butter
1 teaspoon salt
⅛ teaspoon pepper
2 cups rice
⅓ pound Parmesan cheese, grated (about 1½ cups)
½ pound mozzarella
¼ pound cooked ham (about ½ cup)
4 eggs
1½ cups fine, dry bread crumbs
oil

Put water, butter, salt and pepper in large saucepan, bring to boil and add rice. Cover and simmer 20 minutes until rice is tender and water absorbed. Stir in half of Parmesan cheese and let mixture cool. Cut 32 ½-inch cubes from mozzarella and set aside. Mince remaining mozzarella and ham, stir in 2 eggs and remaining Parmesan. Add to cool rice and blend thoroughly. Form into 32 balls, using about ¼ cup rice mixture per ball. Make a small hole in each ball and fill with the ½-inch mozzarella cubes. Re-form ball around cheese cube. Blend the two eggs. Roll rice balls in egg, then in bread crumbs. Place in Cold Cut Keeper until ready to fry, or place half in Snack-Stor and freeze. Thaw before frying. Fry in deep fat at 400°F. until golden brown. Serve at once.

These are delicious – freeze beautifully.

Beirut is a city dedicated to pleasure. Called the "Paris of the Middle East," it has all the ingredients to make an exciting city. There's a fascinating mixture of races from everywhere mingling freely; there's that sweeping vista of the Mediterranean; there are luxury hotels. Food is not the least of Beirut's attractions. Eat European only, if you choose, but what a shame not to sample Middle Eastern dishes! Start out with thimblefuls of Turkish coffee and go on to tackle Mezzeh.

PICNICS

Mezzeh is Beirut's version of non-stop marathon eating . . . as many as 40 dishes. The men sit around for hours engrossed in Mezzeh, conversation, and the hubble-bubble pipe. Stop on your way to Tripoli or Ba'albek and join the picnickers by the side of the road. Try Mezzeh as a different picnic—starting with these dishes. Do not use forks; scoop up food with Arabic bread.

TABBOULEH

5 cups

1 cup fine burghul (crushed wheat)
2 onions, finely chopped (about 1 cup)
1½ teaspoons salt
⅛ teaspoon pepper
1½ cups finely chopped parsley
1 cup lemon juice
¾ cup chopped tomatoes
¾ cup olive oil
½ cup finely chopped fresh mint or
¼ cup dried

Above: Outside of Beirut, the ruins of Ba'albek, an attraction for travelers.

Pour 4 cups boiling water over burghul, let stand about 2 hours. Drain and squeeze through cheesecloth to eliminate all water. Mix burghul, onions, salt and pepper together, crushing onion juice into burghul with fingers. Add remaining ingredients, mix thoroughly. Serve on lettuce leaves in individual dishes or use tender lettuce heart leaves, cabbage leaves and vine leaves as scoops to eat the tabbouleh.

This dish must be served icy cold to be at its best, and tastes much much better if made the day before. Should be kept in a 2-quart Wonderlier.

HUMMUS BI TAHEENI

About 6 cups

2½ cups hummus (chick peas)
½ teaspoon soda
1½ teaspoons salt
1½ cups lemon juice
1 cup taheeni (sesame oil)
¾ cup water
4 cloves garlic, pressed
2 tablespoons chopped parsley
3 tablespoons olive oil
cooked peas

Soak hummus overnight in soda and water to cover. Drain, wash peas well and pick over. Place in pressure cooker, cover with water and add salt. Cook peas 35 minutes under 15 pounds of pressure. Press cooked peas through sieve or put in blender and blend on high speed until smooth. Add lemon juice and taheeni slowly to pea puree, alternately. Add water and garlic. Sauce should be thick and smooth. Stir in olive oil. Place in Party Susan. Garnish with parsley and a few whole cooked peas. Serve icy cold.

Wonderful, well-seasoned appetizer. Could be served in Party Susan with the eggplant (Baba Ghannouj). Both can be frozen and should be served icy cold with flat bread. If you do not have pressure cooker, use 3 cups of canned, cooked chick peas and start at point of putting through sieve.

PARTIES

One of the dividends of travel is the fun you'll have shopping for party accessories. With a Middle Eastern meal, use brass accessories picked up in one of the exotic Oriental bazaars. A small 12-inch brass samovar makes coffee for two or is an attractive centerpiece. Another find: a 4-part oval brass stacking variation of the workmen's lunch box. Fill it with different sweets, set it on the table—unstack at the end of the meal.

KARABEEJ

Makes 40

DOUGH

2 pounds (5 cups) semolina
1½ cups flour
1 pound butter, melted
7 ounces rose water
1 ounce orange water

Sift dry ingredients, add butter and blend thoroughly. Warm orange water and rose water and stir into semolina mixture; knead well. Put into 3-quart Wonderlier, seal tightly and let rest overnight.

SYRUP

4½ cups sugar
2 cups boiling water
3 tablespoons rose water
2 tablespoons lemon juice
1¼ cups honey

Combine sugar, water, rose water, lemon juice in saucepan. Bring to boil, simmer 10 minutes or until thickened. Add honey and remove from heat. Set aside until ready to use.

FILLING

1 tablespoon rose water
1 tablespoon orange water
½ cup superfine sugar
1 cup slivered, blanched almonds

Combine filling ingredients. Knead rested dough. Form about ¼ cup dough into a patty; place 1 teaspoon filling on patty. Put a second patty on top and press sides together to seal well. Round top slightly to form a mound shape. Continue in this manner until all the dough is used up. Place Karabeej on greased cookie sheet. Bake in moderate 350°F. oven for 20 to 25 minutes or until golden. Serve with syrup.

If you have a taste for the rich sweetness of Syrian desserts, these are excellent little cakes. The syrup is very sweet, but the lemon juice and rose water keep it from being too much so, and make the dessert different and interesting. The syrup is wonderfully aromatic.

KATAYEF
PHOENICIA INTER CONTINENTAL

Makes 6 servings

SYRUP

1¼ cups
2 cups sugar
1 cup water
2 tablespoons rose water
2 tablespoons lemon juice

Combine ingredients in saucepan. Bring to a boil, simmer until thickened, about 15 minutes. Store in 2-cup Small Wonderlier.

PANCAKE

Makes 12

1½ cups pancake flour
1¾ cups milk
1 egg
1 tablespoon salad oil

Combine ingredients and stir until well combined. Pour 3 tablespoons batter into a greased 6-inch skillet. Cook until bottom is brown, turn and lightly brown other side. Set aside and cook remaining batter in same manner.

FILLING

1 cup heavy cream
¼ cup confectioners sugar

Whip together until stiff. Put 2 tablespoons cream onto each pancake; fold over and press edges together. Serve with warm syrup.

Delicious dessert pancakes. I am told it is in order to serve these with warm honey or pancake syrup if one is averse to eating rose-flavored syrup. Pancakes can be made ahead and frozen until ready to fill.

HABASH MAHSHI (STUFFED TURKEY)

Serves 12

3 tablespoons oil
3 cups ground meat (about 1¾ pounds)
1½ cups rice
½ cup shelled pine nuts
½ cup shelled pistachio nuts
2 teaspoons salt
1 teaspoon pepper
½ teaspoon cinnamon
1 cup water
¼ cup lemon juice
1 12-pound turkey
¼ pound butter, melted

Heat oil in large skillet. Add meat and cook until brown. Add rice, nuts and spices, stir well. Add liquids; cover and simmer 15 minutes, or until liquids are absorbed. Stuff body and neck of turkey with stuffing. Sew openings tightly with heavy thread. Place bird in a large kettle, add water to barely cover. Add 1 tablespoon salt and bring to boil. Skim. Cover and simmer gently until meat is tender, about 2 hours. Lift the turkey carefully from the kettle and pat dry. Coat with melted butter and place in 450°F. oven until brown, about 15 minutes.

A moist, tender turkey. The stuffing is excellent and most unusual.

SNACKS

At 5 o'clock or after the movies, the Beirut snack bars are jammed with people waiting to sample Shawarma. For Shawarma, mutton or veal is first marinated in vinegar, lemon juice and cardamom seeds and then roasted on a huge spit. Next, meat is cut in thin slices and piled on Arabic bread. Garnish with onions and fresh mint leaves. Mezzeh in the form of any of the recipes that follow also makes excellent Lebanese snacking.

BABA GHANNOUJ

5 cups

3 large eggplants
1¼ cups lemon juice
1 cup taheeni (sesame seed oil)
4 cloves garlic
2 teaspoons salt
parsley
pomegranate seeds
olive oil

Cut stem and green hull from top of eggplant. Bake in 425°F. oven for 1 hour or until flesh is soft and skin crisp. Scoop pulp out of skin. Mash thoroughly. Slowly beat in lemon juice alternately with taheeni. Crush garlic with salt and mix to a paste with a little lemon juice. Blend this into the eggplant mixture. Adjust seasoning to taste. Pour onto shallow dish or Dip-N-Serve dish. Garnish with chopped parsley. Arrange pomegranate seeds in rows across top. Serve surrounded with radishes, green onions and flat bread.

This can be frozen; it dries a little on thawing but one can simply add taheeni by teaspoonfuls until moist enough. Eat by putting on bread or scooping it up on Syrian flat bread.

Picnic and snack on Mezzeh,
Beirut's version of marathon eating.

Below: Shawarma, spit-roasted mutton or veal.

LENTILS MOUDARDARA

9 cups

2 cups lentils (1 14-ounce package)
2 teaspoons salt
4 onions cut into rings then rings cut in halves
1 cup olive oil
1 cup white rice

Wash lentils in cold water. Soak overnight in cold water, in a Handolier. Drain, cover with 5 cups cold water and salt. Bring to a boil, simmer 40 minutes. Sauté onion in oil until soft; add half to lentils with rice. Cover and simmer 30 minutes, or until rice is tender. Chill. Serve garnished with remaining onions. Sprinkle with additional oil if desired.

KABISS (TURNIP PICKLES)

2 quarts

2 pounds turnips
½ pound beets
2¾ cups water
3 tablespoons salt
1 pint white vinegar
1 chili pepper

Wash turnips, peel and wash again; cut in 1-inch cubes. Peel beets and cut into 1-inch cubes. Bring water to a boil, add salt and stir until salt is dissolved. Pour over beets and turnips in a mixing bowl. Add remaining ingredients. Seal and store until desired.

Store in two 30-ounce Square Rounds; cut pepper in half and put half in each. These taste like crunchy Harvard beets.

MELBOURNE

Destination: Melbourne and Sydney, the two largest cities in Australia. Both are cosmopolitan, and both will make the American visitor feel very much at home. In Sydney, swim or surf at some of the finest beaches in the world; Melbourne is memorable particularly for beautiful gardens and parks to visit. Australians enjoy eating, and the food is excellent. Many dishes show their English heritage, but there are typically Australian dishes to be eaten there, duplicated at home.

PICNICS

The Australians take a bounty of beef and oysters and combine them imaginatively at barbecue time. The seasoned oysters snuggle inside the steak to make Carpetbag Steak. Lobster is second to beef in export market, so picnic on cold boiled lobster. With it, Prawn Salad: Mix 2 cups of prawns with 1 cup cooked rice, ½ cup chopped shallots. Season with cream salad dressing.

CARPETBAG STEAK

Serves 4 to 6

2½ pounds boneless sirloin, cut 1½ inches thick
1½ dozen oysters
1 teaspoon salt
¼ teaspoon pepper
2 tablespoons oil
1 tablespoon finely chopped onion
2 teaspoons lemon juice
½ teaspoon paprika
1 tablespoon chopped parsley
2 tablespoons sherry

***Above:** Surfers at Bondi Beach—and Carpetbag Steak.*

Trim surplus fat from steak. Make a slit with sharp knife more than ½ way through to form a pocket. Season pocket with salt and pepper and fill with oysters. Fasten with small skewers or sew with coarse thread. Combine oil, onion, lemon juice and paprika. Place steak in Cold Cut Keeper and cover with oil-lemon juice mixture. Marinate at least 1 hour, turning occasionally. Lightly grease a large frypan and heat. Place steak in pan, lower heat. Cook over moderate heat about 8 to 10 minutes per side for medium rare. Turn once, being careful not to pierce meat. Remove steak from skillet, keep warm. Add marinade and sherry to pan. Bring to boil, stir in parsley, pour over steak.

Unusual, hearty, excellent flavor. Oysters gain much of beef flavor yet retain tender texture; marinade makes delicious sauce.

PARTIES

Emus, parrots and kangaroos are protected under wild life conservation laws now, but there was a time when an Australian party menu from the bush country might read: kangaroo tail stew, braised leg of emu and parrot pie. Now you'll find emus, kangaroos and koalas not on the table but roaming freely in wildlife sanctuaries. In fact, an emu, as you can see, was quick to give his approval to our up-to-date party duck recipe.

An emu inspects Roast Duckling Gold Coast.

BAKED OYSTERS MORNAY

Serves 4 to 6

1 tablespoon butter
1 tablespoon flour
½ cup fish stock or clam juice
¼ cup (1 ounce) grated Gruyere cheese
¼ cup cream
2 tablespoons toasted bread crumbs
2 dozen oysters on half-shell

Melt butter in saucepan. Stir in flour and cook over low heat 2 minutes, being careful not to burn butter. Slowly add fish stock, stirring constantly. Simmer over very low heat, stirring occasionally, for 10 minutes. Add cheese and stir until melted, blend in cream and remove from heat. Arrange the oysters on a bed of rock salt. Spoon sauce over the oysters and sprinkle lightly with the bread crumbs. Bake in 475 °F. oven for about 5 minutes or until the oysters are just cooked through.

ROAST DUCKLING GOLD COAST

Serves 8

2 4-pound ducklings
3 onions, diced
3 carrots diced
1 cup sliced celery
3 tablespoons brandy
½ cup flour
½ cup apple cider
½ cup orange juice
½ cup pineapple juice
½ cup port
1 tablespoon gravy mix
6 slices pineapple

6 apricot halves
6 candied cherries

Wash ducklings inside and out. Remove any extra fat from inside birds; dry well. Place in roasting pan and roast in 325°F. oven for 1 hour. Remove from oven and drain fat into a large skillet. Return duckling to oven for 1½ hours or until done. Meanwhile chop neck, gizzards, duck heart into 1-inch pieces and add to skillet with duck fat. Add vegetables and brown well. Flambé with brandy. Stir in flour, blending well with fat, add liquids gradually, beating constantly. Add 4 cups of water, bring to a boil and skim. Simmer uncovered 1 hour; strain and add gravy mix. Correct for seasoning. Cut cooked duckling into serving pieces and add to gravy. Simmer 10 minutes or until duckling is thoroughly heated. Serve on large platter garnished with fruit.

Rich brown gravy with a pleasant, but not cloyingly sweet, fruit flavor.

PAVLOVA SOUTHERN CROSS

Serves 8

6 egg whites (about ¾ cup)
1½ cups sugar
1½ teaspoons vanilla extract
1½ teaspoons flour
1½ teaspoons vinegar
1 pint heavy cream, whipped
sliced fresh fruit (raspberries, strawberries, bananas, or pears) well drained

Beat egg whites until foamy. Gradually beat in sugar, a little at a time. Beat until stiff and glossy. Fold in vanilla, flour and vinegar. Spread mixture into a well-greased 10-inch round cake pan, making sides about 1-inch higher than center. Place in a 325°F. oven for 1 hour. The Pavlova should be crisp and golden brown on surface and soft inside. When cold, fill with whipped cream and place drained fruit on top. If desired, Pavlova may be removed from baking pan before being filled and placed in Pie Taker. The meringue may be frozen this way or filled and then frozen (bananas do not freeze.)

A crispy yet tender meringue, a very attractive and impressive dessert. If frozen, the meringue should be removed from freezer 1 hour before serving.

SNACKS

Pie 'n' Sauce is the national snack, and it's as popular in Australia as hot dogs are here. The "pie" will usually be an individual-size serving filled with a variety of meats — try beef or lamb. The "sauce" is ketchup. Eat Pie 'n' Sauce at any of the sporting events the Australians are addicted to — championship tennis, for example — or after watching Lawn Bowls or marveling at the surfers at Bondi Beach in Sydney.

PIE 'N' SAUCE CURRIED LAMB PIE

Serves 6

¼ cup butter
2 onions, chopped (about 1 cup)

Tasty Down-Under snack: Pie 'n' Sauce.

2 pounds lean lamb cut in ½-inch cubes
2 cups milk
½ cup grated coconut
2 tablespoons curry powder
1 tablespoon ground ginger
2 teaspoons salt
⅛ teaspoon pepper
½ cup cream
1 tablespoon lemon juice
pastry for 1 9-inch pie

Melt 2 tablespoons butter in large skillet. Add onions and sauté until tender. Add remaining butter and lamb and brown meat on all sides. Add milk, coconut and spices; mix well. Simmer, covered, 45 minutes or until meat is tender. Add cream and lemon juice and simmer uncovered 15 minutes. (Mixture will appear slightly curdled.) Spoon curry into six 1½-cup baking dishes; cover each with pastry. Slit pastry to allow steam to escape. Bake in 425°F. oven 15 to 20 minutes or until pastry is brown. May be served with chutney, coconut or chopped nuts.

PIE 'N' SAUCE BEEF PIE

6 Servings

½ cup flour
½ teaspoon salt
¾ pound stew beef, cut into 1-inch pieces
2½ tablespoons bacon fat
1 package (¾ ounce) brown gravy mix
1 cup beef stock
¼ cup apple cider
2 medium onions, chopped
2 carrots, cut into ½-inch cubes
1 tablespoon chopped parsley
1 bay leaf
⅛ teaspoon thyme
⅛ teaspoon pepper
1 clove garlic, crushed
double crust for 9-inch pie

Combine flour and salt, use to coat beef cubes. Heat bacon fat in large saucepan. Add beef cubes and brown on all sides. Stir in gravy mix and remaining flour-salt mix. Add stock gradually, stirring constantly, until flour and gravy mix are well blended and liquid is smooth. Add everything but pie crust. Cook over moderate heat 1½ hours or until meat is tender. Divide crust in half, fit half into bottom and up the sides of an 8-inch cake pan. Fill with cooled meat mixture. Moisten top edge of pastry with water. Top with remaining pastry, press together to seal well. Bake in 400°F. oven 50 minutes.

Bangkok

This is a city that won't disappoint you. Bangkok's fairyland architecture of many-spired temples and palaces will hold you spellbound. And there's the Floating Market, easily the most fascinating place in the world to visit. And there are the people—all of them utterly charming. The beautiful colorings of Thai silks—turquoise, Siam pink, lacquer yellow—give you the feeling of being surrounded by a rainbow.

PICNICS

Thais don't picnic in our sense, but we did find recipes that could easily adapt to outdoor entertaining. There's an abundance of fruit in Thailand. Try several kinds of banana, papaya, young coconut and sakay (breadfruit). Delicious and elegant Thai version of fruit cup, Crown of Fruit, is easy to make and very refreshing poolside or on a hot summer's night.

THAI CROWN OF FRUIT

Cut a large slice, about 4 inches, off the top of a melon (papaya, honeydew or cantaloupe). Cut triangles within ½ inch of bottom of melon to create a crown effect. Hollow out center and fill with: banana slices cut in quarters, cut-up reserved melon, small pieces of pineapple and whatever other fruits you prefer. In Bangkok, "Crown of Fruit" is garnished with lotus nuts. You can substitute macadamias or cashews. Optional: marinate cut-up fruit in brandy for several hours. Fruit Crowns can be carried on a picnic in a Square Keeper.

PARTIES

Thais have distinctive table accessories that complement the richness of their food, but that would also enhance any Eastern party food you might be serving. Characteristic is a low wooden table surrounded with brilliant silk pillows to sit on. Or concentrate on table-top decor. Use hand-painted lacquer plates, heavily decorated bronze flatware and, for a centerpiece, one of the many interesting carved and gilded figures.

KUNG NAO (SHRIMPS IN WINTER)

Serves 6 to 8

24 small shrimp (about ½ pound)
2 teaspoons monosodium glutamate
24 very thin slices of bread
1 egg, slightly beaten
Sweet and Sour Sauce (recipe below)

Clean and shell shrimp, sprinkle with monosodium glutamate. Remove crusts from bread; wrap shrimp in slices, seal with beaten egg. Fry in medium hot fat (375°F.) until brown — about 5 minutes, or until shrimp are cooked. Remove to paper to drain. Serve with Sweet and Sour Sauce.

SWEET AND SOUR SAUCE

1⅓ cups sauce

1 large dried mushroom
2 tablespoons chopped scallions
2 tablespoons chopped mixed pickle
2 tablespoons flour
½ cup vinegar
½ cup soy sauce
½ cup water
⅓ cup sugar

Soak mushroom to soften, wash thoroughly and chop. Combine with scallions and pickle and place in saucepan. Blend flour with vinegar to form a smooth paste; add with remaining ingredients to mushroom-scallion mixture. Cook over moderate heat, stirring occasionally, until sauce is thickened.

Excellent sort of an easy-do egg roll to serve as an appetizer.

PU CHA (STUFFED CRAB)

Serves 4

4 boiled hardshell crabs
½ teaspoon garlic powder
¼ teaspoon ground coriander
¼ teaspoon soy sauce
⅛ teaspoon ground pepper
1 egg, separated
¼ cup heavy cream, whipped

Remove meat from crab; combine with garlic powder, coriander, soy, pepper, beaten egg white and whipped cream. Fill cleaned crab shells with the mixture. Brush top with slightly beaten egg yolk. Place in steamer, over boiling water, steam 10 minutes, cool. Store in Snack-Stor until ready to fry. Before serving, fry filled crabs in deep, hot (400°F.) fat until brown, about 1 minute.

Serve as an appetizer-first course. This is an easy-to-do dish, since most preparation up to frying can be done early in morning.

KAENG PHED (MEAT CURRY)

Serves 5 to 6

2 tablespoons oil
2½ pounds beef, cut in 1-inch cubes
4 cups coconut cream (recipe below)
curry paste (recipe below)
1 teaspoon flour
green chilies

Heat oil in large skillet. Add beef and brown on all sides. Add coconut cream and bring mixture to a boil. Turn heat down and simmer 40 minutes or until meat is almost done. Skim fat from top of liquid, stir in curry paste and cook another 20 minutes. Mixture will appear slightly curdled at this point. Pour a small amount of gravy over flour in a Sauce Dish, mix to a paste. Return to curry and blend well. Cook another 2 minutes or until curry thickens slightly. Stir in green chilies according to degree of hotness desired.

COCONUT CREAM

4 cups

2 cups milk
2 cups heavy cream
1 cup water
1 teaspoon salt
1⅓ cup flaked coconut (1 4-ounce can)

Combine liquids, salt, coconut in saucepan. Bring to a boil; reduce heat, simmer 10 minutes. Pour through sieve, discard coconut.

CURRY PASTE

2 tablespoons chopped shallot
2 tablespoons lemon juice
1 tablespoon ground coriander
2 cloves garlic, minced
2 teaspoons chopped chili peppers
2 teaspoons grated lemon rind
2 teaspoons ground turmeric
1 teaspoon salt
1 teaspoon cinnamon

Blend all ingredients to a fine paste.

A different curry, more creamy than the Indian type. The amount of "hot" in a curry really depends on the amount of chili peppers used.

SNACKS

The klons are Thailand's winding system of canals near Bangkok. Houses, with steps leading right into the water, line either side of the canals and sarong-clad men, women and children are everywhere, at work and at play. On the klons, you'll find the floating market with dozens of boats filled with fresh fruits and vegetables. Other boats serve the snack food Thais enjoy. Sample noodles or rice Chinese style, or tasty Thai curry.

ROAST RIBS OF PORK SIAM INTER CONTINENTAL

Serves 6 to 8

4 to 5 pound pork loin roast
1 large pineapple

2 tablespoons ground coriander
2 cloves garlic, pressed
1 teaspoon ground pepper
1 teaspoon salt
¼ cup sugar
2 tablespoons vinegar
2 tablespoons soy sauce
2 cucumbers
red chilies

Insert a pointed knife in roast along the ribs and cut close, stopping at the end of the bones, so that the meat is held to the end of the bones. Thrust two or three flat sticks in between the bones and the meat to hold the meat up above the bones. Peel the pineapple; reserve the rind and set aside the flesh for decoration. Combine the coriander, garlic, pepper and salt, rub over meat. Place meat on flat roasting pan and cover with the pineapple rind. Bake, fat side up, in a 350°F. oven for 2 hours. Combine sugar, vinegar and soy and sprinkle over loin. Bake another half hour or until pork reaches 185°F. on meat thermometer. Baste once or twice during this remaining half hour with soy mixture. Remove roast from oven and skim fat from roasting pan. Stir any remaining soy mixture into pan gravy and heat. Use pineapple and cucumbers cut into pieces and red chilies to form flowers over the roast. Serve gravy over decorated roast.

Pineapple and cucumber excellent combination with the pork. Has an elusively oriental flavor, very attractive; crust of roast is crunchy, delicious.

At Bangkok's floating market.

Hong Kong

Hong Kong is more than a shopper's mecca. It is gaily cosmopolitan, with towering modern buildings, fountain-filled squares and English tea at 4 o'clock. That's one side of Hong Kong. The other exists on the water. Aberdeen Fishing Village is one place you'll see Hong Kong as a bustling water city filled with junks and sampans and pajama-clad women. Hong Kong has contrasts, too, in the food you'll eat. Our recipes reflect the best of both Chinese and fine continental food.

PICNICS

From Hong Kong there are many excursion possibilities; the beach at Repulse Bay, the New Territories, the island of Macao—any or all reason enough for a picnic Hong Kong style. Order food cooked in the morning, pack it in Tupperware, eat it while it is still warm. Why not a Chinese picnic at your home town beach or park? What excitement you'll create!

COLD CHICKEN WINGS WITH BROWN SAUCE

10 wings

3 tablespoons Chinese wine or dry sherry
1 tablespoon salt
1 teaspoon ground pepper
2 pounds (about 10) chicken wings
½ stalk leek, cut into small pieces
4 slices ginger (or 1 teaspoon powdered ginger)
5 tablespoons soy sauce
3 tablespoons sesame oil
1 tablespoon sugar

Mix wine, salt and pepper, rub into wings. Cover with leek and ginger and steam over high heat 30 minutes. Heat soy, sesame oil, sugar and 1 cup juice from steaming liquid. Add chicken wings, 3 at a time, bring to a boil, turning constantly until color changes. Cool wings and store in 2-quart Wonderlier.

Though chicken wings are not usually my cup of tea these have a piquant and appealing flavor and are just different enough to be interesting.

FRIED NOODLES WITH ASSORTED MEAT

Serves 8

¾ pound very fine egg noodles
½ cup oil
¼ teaspoon finely chopped fresh ginger (or ⅛ teaspoon powdered ginger)
1 scallion, chopped
¼ pound pork, finely shredded
¼ pound sliced chicken
2 abalone, sliced
½ pound small shrimp, shelled and cleaned
½ teaspoon soy sauce
½ teaspoon Chinese wine or dry sherry
⅛ teaspoon salt
⅛ teaspoon monosodium glutamate
5 dried mushrooms soaked, sliced and cooked
¼ pound bamboo shoots
½ package frozen peas
¼ pound ham
1 cup chicken stock
⅓ cup Chinese wine or dry sherry
¼ cup soy sauce

Veal Cutlets Kublai Khan – if you can't have them in Hong Kong, do the second-best thing – have them at home.

½ teaspoon salt

1½ teaspoons cornstarch with
2 tablespoons water

¼ teaspoon monosodium glutamate

Fry noodles in ¼ cup hot oil until light brown, set aside. Heat remaining oil in large frypan, add ginger and fry until light brown; remove from oil and discard. Brown scallion in oil. Combine soy sauce, wine, salt, monosodium glutamate. Sprinkle over meat and fish and blend well. Add to scallion and fry 2 to 3 minutes. Add mushrooms, bamboo shoots, peas and ham, and bring to a boil. Add remaining ingredients and simmer 5 minutes. Blend with noodles and store in 3-quart Wonderlier. If desired, half may be used immediately and the other half frozen.

PARTIES

At a Hong Kong party, you'll be served both Chinese and Western food. "Small chow" is the hors d'oeuvre version of egg roll, bamboo shoots, etc., you will be served first. Then the meal could take a Western turn with dishes such as Veal Cutlets Kublai Khan. Also popular are Sunday curry lunches and launch parties—the latter, aboard a friend's boat, start with a cruise to work up an appetite for a festive lunch.

PALM HEART SALAD

Serves 8

1 apple, chopped (about 1 cup)

2 tablespoons lemon juice

½ teaspoon salt

1 cup mayonnaise

2 tablespoons chopped pistachio nuts

2 tablespoons rum

1 tablespoon heavy cream

1 14-ounce can hearts of palm
(4 palm hearts)

Combine apple, lemon juice and salt in a 2-cup Wonderlier, marinate 1 hour. Combine mayonnaise, nuts, rum, cream in another container; drain apples and add to mayonnaise mixture. Cut each palm heart in half and place on serving plates. Cover with mayonnaise sauce.

An excellent, tangy sauce, very good with the palm hearts. Makes 2 cups sauce. Can be made ahead and stored in refrigerator several days.

VEAL CUTLETS KUBLAI KHAN

Serves 5

5 8-ounce veal rib chops

⅓ cup lemon juice

4 mint leaves, chopped

3 ounces chicken liver

½ cup (1 stick) butter

2 ounces foie gras

1 ounce cooked ham, chopped

5 eggs, fried

Marinate veal in lemon juice and mint in Snack-Stor for 1 hour. Sauté chicken livers in 2 tablespoons butter for 5 to 10 minutes, or until inside is no longer pink. Mix with foie gras and ham and 1 tablespoon butter. Remove chops from marinade and dry well. Cut a slit in the muscle of each chop; fill with the pâté mixture, secure with toothpicks. Melt remaining butter in large frypan. Add chops and sauté 5 minutes on each side or until done. Place cooked veal on serving plate and top each with a fried egg. Serve with boiled potatoes garnished with chopped red pimientos.

BEEF IN OYSTER SAUCE

Serves 2

2 tablespoons oil
1 tablespoon cornstarch
½ teaspoon bicarbonate of soda
½ teaspoon salt
½ teaspoon monosodium glutamate
½ teaspoon ginger juice
½ teaspoon Chinese wine
½ teaspoon soy sauce
½ pound boneless steak, cut into thin slices
½ cup water
½ teaspoon white vinegar
1 pound lard

GRAVY INGREDIENTS

1 tablespoon stock
1 tablespoon oyster sauce
½ teaspoon sugar
½ teaspoon monosodium glutamate
½ teaspoon cornstarch
½ teaspoon soy sauce
½ teaspoon sesame oil

VEGETABLES

4 white mushrooms, cooked, quartered
3 stalks scallion, cut in 1-inch sections
3 thin slices ginger
1 clove garlic, minced

Combine first eight ingredients and knead into thinly sliced beef. This is easiest to do in the Pie Taker to conserve ingredients, and give room to knead. Add water a tablespoon at a time, kneading constantly until all liquid is worked into meat. Let stand for one hour, stir in vinegar. Heat saucepan, put in lard. When hot, add beef and simmer 3 to 4 minutes or until meat changes color; remove from fat. (Recipe may be prepared to this point and set aside until ready to serve. Gravy ingredients and vegetables may be combined in a Square Round and held until cooking time.) In large frypan heat 1 tablespoon of the lard. Stir in gravy ingredients and vegetables and beef; cook until heated throughout. Add 1 more tablespoon lard, mix well and serve.

A very good, very authentic Chinese dish. All foods can be prepared ahead and then combined at last minute. Can be stored in the 30-ounce Square Round.

CHICKEN AND SWEET CORN SOUP

Serves 6 to 8

1½ teaspoons soy sauce
1 teaspoon salt
1 teaspoon monosodium glutamate
½ teaspoon pepper
½ teaspoon Chinese wine or dry sherry
6 ounces chicken breast, chopped fine
2 egg whites, slightly beaten
1½ tablespoons oil
3 cups chicken bouillon
1 12-ounce can corn
4 teaspoons cornstarch
3 tablespoons water

Combine ½ teaspoon soy sauce, ½ teaspoon salt, ½ teaspoon monosodium glutamate, pepper, and wine; rub into chicken pieces. Add egg whites and blend well, set aside. Heat oil in large

saucepan, add bouillon and corn. Bring to boil and boil 5 minutes. Combine cornstarch and water to make smooth paste; add the soup and mix well. Add chicken-egg white mixture and simmer gently until chicken is cooked and soup thickened. Season.

A very tasty, hearty, unusual soup.

DRIED MUSHROOMS

2 ounces dried black mushrooms (sometimes called Chinese Mushrooms or Fragrant Mushrooms)

Above, left: Lobster and crab dinners come straight from waters alongside the Floating Restaurants. Above, right: picnic fare, Chinese style.

¾ cup water
1 tablespoon melted lard
½ teaspoon salt

Soak mushrooms in water to cover for 15 minutes. Cut off stems. Simmer mushrooms, in the water to which the lard and salt have been added, for 30 minutes. Drain and use.

SHRIMPS BAHAMAS

Serves 3 to 4

1 pound peeled, deveined shrimp
2 tablespoons olive oil
2 tablespoons butter
¼ cup Irish whiskey
½ teaspoon flour
¼ cup cream
¼ cup fish stock
1 tablespoon curry powder
2 slices fresh pineapple, cut in large pieces
2 bananas, cut in ½-inch slices

Marinate the raw shrimp in oil, in 30-ounce Square Round, for 3 hours. Melt butter in large saucepan. Add shrimp, sauté slowly for 2 to 3 minutes. Add whiskey and flambé. Sprinkle with flour and stir to blend. Add remaining ingredients, simmer 10 minutes. Serve with rice.

A very unusual curry—the bananas give it a sweet flavor totally different from any other curry we have tried. Drained shrimp may be held overnight after marinating, cooked next day.

LOBSTER CORAL BAY

Serves 4

1½ pounds lobster meat
3 tablespoons butter
2 tablespoons brandy
1 teaspoon flour
1 cup sour cream
1 10-ounce package frozen spinach, cooked
½ cup cooked peas
¼ cup chopped cooked carrots
1 cup hollandaise sauce
1 tablespoon Parmesan cheese

Cut lobster meat into large pieces, sauté gently in butter. Pour on brandy and flambé. Add flour, stir until combined with butter. Add sour cream and vegetables, simmer 10 minutes, stirring occasionally. Remove from heat and stir in hollandaise. Pour into a 1½-quart casserole. Sprinkle with cheese and bake in a 450°F. oven until heated through, about 10 minutes. Serve with rice.

PORK FILLET ZIO MANDY

Serves 8 to 10

2 pounds boneless pork fillets
2 leeks
2 tablespoons Dijon mustard
4 ounces diced ham
2 tablespoons flour
2 tablespoons butter
½ cup white wine
½ cup chicken stock or broth
1 clove garlic
1 onion, sliced
1 carrot, minced
1 teaspoon salt
½ cup heavy cream

Slit the pork fillets lengthwise down the middle, but do not cut all the way through. Wash and split the leeks, lay down the center of the fillets. Fold meat around leeks and tie in several places to secure roll. Spread mustard over surface of pork. Wrap a slice of ham around pork and wrap the fillet in aluminum foil. Place in broiler for 10 minutes, then roast in 350°F. oven for 1½ hours, or until meat thermometer reads 185°F. Melt butter in a saucepan; add flour and stir over medium heat 5 minutes. Gradually add the wine and stock, stirring constantly. Add vegetables and simmer 25 minutes; strain. Add salt and cream and return to heat. Bring to a simmer, serve over pork.

SPIT-ROASTED LAMB MANDARIN STYLE

Serves 8 to 10

⅓ cup butter
½ pound calves' liver
2 cups fresh white bread crumbs
¼ cup raisins
1 egg, slightly beaten
1 clove garlic, finely minced
¼ cup minced parsley
½ teaspoon salt
¼ teaspoon ground thyme
¼ teaspoon ground pepper
1 6-pound leg of lamb, boned
salt
paprika
chopped mint leaves
oil

Melt 2 tablespoons butter in frypan. Add liver, sauté a few minutes until outside is brown but inside is still pink. Remove from pan and mince well. Melt remaining butter and combine with liver, breadcrumbs, raisins, egg, garlic, parsley, ½ teaspoon salt, thyme and pepper. Lay the boned lamb, skin side down, on a flat surface. Spread the stuffing over the meat and into the pockets left by the bones. Roll the meat into a cylindrical shape to hold all the stuffing. Close the opening with needle and thread. Rub the lamb completely with salt, paprika, and mint leaves. Rub oil liberally over the whole outside. Place on spit and roast slowly over an open charcoal fire for about 1 to 1½ hours, depending on heat of fire. If desired, roast in 350°F. oven about 1 to 1¼ hours for medium rare.

An excellent recipe, filling is one of the best I have tasted.

WALNUT CHICKEN

Serves 2 to 3

4 ounces walnuts
1 pound lard
12 ounces chicken meat, diced
2 thin slices ginger (or ½ teaspoon powdered ginger)
3 stalks scallion, cut into sections
3 mushrooms, cut into quarters
1 clove garlic, minced

CHICKEN SEASONING INGREDIENTS

1 egg white
1 teaspoon cornstarch
½ teaspoon Chinese wine or dry sherry
⅛ teaspoon salt
⅛ teaspoon pepper
⅛ teaspoon monosodium glutamate

GRAVY INGREDIENTS

2 tablespoons chicken stock or broth
1 tablespoon oyster sauce
½ teaspoon cornstarch, mixed with 1 tablespoon water
½ teaspoon soy sauce
⅛ teaspoon sesame oil

Boil walnuts in slightly salted water for 10 minutes, strain. Place lard in large frypan, heat to melt. Add walnuts and cook over low flame 20 minutes, then bring lard to boil and boil for 1 minute. This makes nuts very crispy. Combine chicken seasoning ingredients, mix into chicken. Heat lard again; when very hot (400°F.) add chicken. Remove from heat and stir gently half a minute. Remove chicken from lard. In large frypan put 1 tablespoon lard. Add vegetables and gravy ingredients and chicken, simmer until all ingredients are hot. Add walnuts, mix well. Serve with rice.

Excellent—nuts are surprisingly tasty, very crunchy, not at all bitter, as walnuts are apt to be.

SNACKS

There are no typical Chinese snacks in Hong Kong—just whatever appeals to individual tastes. After the movies, a concert, or a lecture at the University on archaeological finds or ancient history of Hong Kong, people are likely to stop for French Onion Soup or hamburgers. Since the Chinese have a real sweet tooth, they're also fond of eating rich pastries along with the coffee served at International Coffee Houses.

EGGS COOKED WITH TEA LEAVES

10 eggs
2 tablespoons black tea
2 teaspoons salt
1 teaspoon black pepper
10 aniseeds
⅓ cup soy sauce

Place eggs in pan, cover with water and bring to a boil, simmer 10 minutes. Soak in cold water and crack all over with a spoon, but keep shell on egg. Add remaining ingredients to water and cook eggs again, this time for 20 minutes. Remove from heat and shell. The resulting pattern is lovely. Store in a 4-cup Wonderlier.

ROQUEFORT ROULADES

50 hors d' oeuvres

5 ounce Roquefort cheese
4 tablespoons butter
1 ounce anchovy fillets
3 hard-cooked eggs, chopped
¼ cup finely chopped parsley
10 slices cold roast beef

Blend cheese, butter and anchovies to a smooth paste. Blend in eggs and parsley. Spread the beef slices with the cheese mixture and roll as for a jelly roll. Place in 1-pound Cheese Saver and refrigerate at least 1 hour. Slice each roll in 5 pieces and serve.

Aberdeen fishing village—Sweet and Sour Fish.

SWEET AND SOUR FISH

Serves 4

1 tablespoon soy sauce
1 tablespoon Chinese wine or dry sherry
1 egg
¾ pound sea bass or pike
2 tablespoons cornstarch
1 pound lard

Mix soy, wine and egg. Cut fish into 1-inch cubes and coat with egg mixture. Sprinkle cornstarch over fish and coat thoroughly. Heat lard and add fish; fry 3 to 5 minutes or until fish is just cooked. Remove from heat and serve at once with Sweet and Sour Sauce.

SWEET AND SOUR SAUCE

½ cup white vinegar
⅓ cup sugar
2 tablespoons cornstarch
¼ cup bamboo shoots
2 tablespoons pineapple juice
2 tablespoons ketchup
1 teaspoon soy sauce
5 crab apples, cored and cut in large pieces
½ green pepper, cut into long slices
3 pineapple slices, cut into eigths
1 small clove garlic, minced
1 tablespoon lard

Combine sugar and cornstarch, stir in remaining ingredients. Cook over moderate heat, stirring occasionally, until liquid is slightly thickened and ingredients heated thoroughly. Pour over fish and serve hot. Serve with rice, if desired.

FRIED RICE WITH ASSORTED MEAT

Serves 8 to 10

¾ cup oil
5 eggs
¼ pound shrimp, shelled and cleaned
¼ pound chicken meat (1 breast) cooked and diced
¼ pound roast pork, diced
6 dried mushrooms, soaked and cooked
¼ pound frozen peas (½ package) cooked
8 cups cooked rice
¼ cup chicken stock
3 tablespoons soy sauce
2 tablespoons Chinese wine or dry sherry
salt
pepper

Heat 3 tablespoons oil in frypan; beat 3 eggs and cook in oil. Break into small pieces and remove to a plate. Add another 3 tablespoons oil to pan, add shrimp and fry quickly. Add remaining meats, mushrooms, and peas; sauté 2 minutes and set aside. Combine remaining ingredients except oil in Fix-N-Mix. Add cooked meat mixture and mix until completely blended. In large skillet heat remaining oil. Stir in rice mixture and sauté two or three minutes, until eggs are firm. Cool and season to taste. If desired, half of mixture may be placed in a 2-quart Wonderlier and frozen.

This is excellent fried rice. It makes a large amount but since it freezes so well and takes a bit of time to make, it makes sense to make a big batch and freeze half for a quick lunch dish at a future date.

Manila is one Far Eastern city with which most Americans feel a kinship. From the time you arrive and are greeted with "Mabuhay," the Tagalog equivalent of "welcome," you feel at home. The city is just revitalizing itself after the destruction of the last war. Visit Intramuros, the old Spanish Walled City, now in ruins, to get the flavor of the old; for a look at the Manila of the future, go to the Makati section, Manila's new, booming area of glass-walled skyscrapers.

PICNICS

A short drive from Manila, there are two beautiful picnic sites. By all means, rent a jeepney—those unique-to-Manila jazzed-up jeeps. Drive one hour to Tagatay, site of Taal Lake and Volcano. Or go two hours to Matabungkay. Rent a small cottage on the beach, swim, loaf and picnic. Use banana leaves that you will pick from a nearby tree for plates, and eat Pancit.

PANCIT

Serves 10 to 12

PANCIT

1 pound dried rice noodles
1 cup bean sprouts, boiled
½ cup flaked smoked fish (tinapa)
½ cup crisp cracklings or bacon rind, pounded
2 hard-cooked eggs, chopped
½ cup shelled, cooked shrimp
½ cup finely sliced scallions
1 lemon, thinly sliced
patis (fish sauce)

Bring 2 quarts of water to boil in a deep pan. Put a handful of noodles into a strainer and dip into boiling water for 1 minute. Drain well. Continue until all the noodles have been cooked. Combine with cooked sprouts in bottom of Fix-N-Mix. Pour thin sauce (Palabok) over the noodles. Top with the pork and bean curd sauce. Sprinkle with remaining ingredients plus reserved garlic.

PALABOK

2 cups pork stock
½ cup water
½ cup flour
1 teaspoon monosodium glutamate
1 teaspoon salt

Pour stock into large saucepan. Add water to flour to make a smooth paste, add to pork stock. Add remaining ingredients, bring mixture to a boil. Simmer, stirring occasionally, until slightly thickened, about 5 minutes.

PANCIT LUG-LUG

3½ cups sauce

3 tablespoons cooking oil
3 cloves garlic, minced
1 cup diced, cooked pork
2 cakes bean curd (two 8¾-ounce cans), diced
1 cup pork stock
½ cup Chinese celery, cut into 1-inch pieces
1 teaspoon salt
1 teaspoon monosodium glutamate

Heat oil in large frypan. Add garlic and cook until brown. Remove garlic and set aside for garnishing. Add pork and sauté until slightly brown. Add bean curd, sauté 1 minute. Add stock and bring to a boil. Add remaining ingredients; simmer 1 minute more. Set aside.

PARTIES

The Filipinos are gregarious and hospitable. They love to party and qualify as excellent dancers. With all the festiveness, there is still a relaxed informality. Ties and jackets are rarely required. Instead, the men wear elaborately embroidered jacket-shirts, the barong tagalog. Even party food is uncomplicated. Most popular is Adobo—our fresh ham recipe, a variation on the usual chicken-and-pork Adobo, is a delicious at-home party dish.

PORK ADOBO

Serves 16

8-pound fresh ham
2 cups cider vinegar
1 cup soy sauce
2 teaspoons salt
1½ teaspoons pepper
6 cloves garlic, finely minced

Place pork in Square Keeper; combine remaining ingredients and pour over pork. Marinate one hour. Place pork and marinade in large covered roasting pan, add 6 cups water. Simmer, covered, until tender, about 4 hours. Strain sauce; reduce, by boiling in an open pan, to 3 cups. Skim fat and set gravy aside. Pour 3 tablespoons skimmed fat into large pan; add pork and brown on all sides. Add gravy, simmer 20 minutes.

UKOY SHRIMP FRITTER

Makes 12 fritters

1 cup water
1 cup cornstarch
2 eggs, well beaten
1 onion, chopped
1 cup drained bean sprouts
½ pound ground pork
1 teaspoon salt
4 cups cooking oil
½ pound shelled small shrimp
¼ cup vinegar
2 cloves garlic, minced

Gradually add water to cornstarch to make a smooth paste. Stir in eggs, mix well. Add onion, bean sprouts, pork and salt; mix well. Heat oil in a deep frypan. Pour ¼ cup batter into hot oil, lay 2 or 3 shrimp on surface. Fry until fritter is golden. Serve with garlic vinegar: combine vinegar and garlic in Sauce Dish, let stand for at least 2 hours.

Tupperware makes food transport easy. Right: a Filipino snack table—Ukoy Shrimp, Lumpia, and accompaniments.

SNACKS

Merienda, the Filipino idea of a 5 p.m. snack, is no light repast. It can be as simple as tea and pastries, but more often goes on to many dishes. Hot chocolate, a preference dating back to Spanish occupation, may also be served. We like the idea of a summertime merienda served outdoors with iced tea made quickly and perfectly from a mix. Arrange, if you can, a dazzling sunset, similar to the spectaculars over Manila Bay.

LUMPIA

Serves 6 to 8

FILLING

4½ cups filling

4 large cloves garlic, minced
1 onion, chopped
2 tablespoons cooking oil
1 pound ground pork
½ pound shelled shrimp, chopped
1½ cups (1 4-ounce can) southern style coconut
1½ teaspoons salt
1 teaspoon monosodium glutamate
1 teaspoon sugar

Sauté garlic and onion in the oil until tender. Add pork; sauté, stirring occasionally, until completely cooked. Add the shrimp and continue cooking until they turn pink. Add coconut, cook over low heat 2 more minutes. Add remaining ingredients, stir well and remove from heat. Cool before wrapping. Store in 2-quart Wonderlier.

WRAPPER

18 Wrappers

1½ cups water
¾ cup cornstarch
3 eggs, well beaten
¾ teaspoon salt
5 teaspoons cooking oil

Gradually add water to cornstarch to make a smooth paste. Add remaining ingredients, mix well. Brush a 6-inch skillet with oil. Pour about 3 tablespoons batter into pan, tipping to coat with a thin layer of batter. Cook until surface begins to bubble. Remove and set aside. When all are cooked, place about ¼ cup filling on each wrapper, fold over and serve with sauce.

LUMPIA SAUCE

3 cups

2 cloves garlic, crushed
1 tablespoon cooking oil
4 tablespoons cornstarch
⅓ cup brown sugar
2½ cups water
½ cup soy sauce

Sauté garlic in oil until brown. Remove from pan. Combine cornstarch and sugar. Add remaining ingredients, blend thoroughly. Pour into pan in which garlic was cooked. Simmer, stirring constantly, until thickened. Remove from heat and serve, topped with garlic, over Lumpia.

Filling can also be wrapped in lettuce leaves – different texture but very good.

If you're adventurous, you'll find Singapore filled with tempting food ideas. Small wonder, since there are many different national foods to be savored. There's Chinese and Malay food, Javanese Rijsttafel, Indian curries, to name only a few. Try them all if you have time. Start with Satay at your hotel. Go another night to the eating stalls, or take the side trip that features dinner in an orchid-scented garden, an evening that ends with a delightful program of native dances.

PICNICS

Indonesian Satay is one of those adaptable recipes that could be the basis for a party, picnic or snack. Serve Satay as a snack after a game of tennis or a cooling swim. Make it the star of "grill your own hors d'oeuvres" at a Patio Party. But perhaps Satay is most unusual at a picnic. Transport the makings in a Snack-Stor. Grill, serve with sauce on a Dip-N-Serve tray.

Above: Steamboat is a guest-participation specialty—gets its name from its cooking pot.

CHICKEN SATAY

Serves 4

1 clove garlic, chopped
¼ cup cooking oil
¼ cup soy sauce
1 tablespoon chopped onion
1 teaspoon sugar
⅛ teaspoon curry powder
1 3-pound chicken, boned, skinned, cut into bite-size pieces
Satay Sauce (recipe below)

Combine garlic, oil, soy sauce,

onion, sugar, curry and mix to a fine paste; coat chicken thoroughly with this paste. Place in 4-cup Wonderlier, store in refrigerator for 24 hours. Remove from refrigerator and place 5 small pieces of chicken on each of as many skewers as needed. Brush meat with oil and put on charcoal broiler. Turn and baste with oil several times during cooking. Cook about 10 minutes or until chicken is done. Serve with Satay Sauce.

SATAY SAUCE

2 cups

1 clove garlic, minced
2 onions, minced
½ cup minced pineapple
½ teaspoon finely minced fresh ginger (or ¼ teaspoon ground ginger)
1 small chili pepper, minced
3 tablespoons peanut butter
¾ cup grated coconut
¾ cup coconut milk (liquid from 1 coconut)
½ cup chicken stock
2 tablespoons sugar
½ teaspoon curry powder
½ teaspoon salt
¼ teaspoon garlic powder
¼ teaspoon pepper

Combine first 5 ingredients. Heat peanut butter in saucepan, add combined ingredients and set aside. Combine grated coconut and coconut liquid; bring to boil in small saucepan. Remove from heat and sieve. Combine with all ingredients and simmer over moderate heat 15 minutes. Do not strain. If sauce is too thick, more chicken stock may be added. This may be stored, refrigerated or frozen, until ready to use.

Chicken has an excellent flavor with or without sauce. This is a relatively hot curry, so be careful.

There are outdoor eating stalls everywhere.

PARTIES

Two unusual Singapore party dishes: One, Chicken Singapura, is a Westernized version of an Oriental dish. The pineapple "ducks" used as servers were an inspiration of the chef, one you can omit if you don't feel artistic. Steamboat, named after the pot that is used, is the other party recipe. Here's a dish that is fun for the hostess! The guests cook their own dinner, enjoy every minute, and leave praising your cooking talents.

CHICKEN WITH GREEN RICE SINGAPURA INTER CONTINENTAL

Serves 3 to 4

2 tablespoons butter
1 pound chicken meat, cut in small pieces
1 tablespoon chopped shallots
1 teaspoon minced garlic
3 ounces dried mushrooms, cooked
¾ cup brown gravy
¼ cup white wine

Melt butter in a frypan. Add

chicken and sauté until it browns on all sides. Add shallots and garlic and sauté until soft. Add remaining ingredients; simmer 10 minutes, or until chicken is cooked. Serve with pan-fried pineapple ring, if desired. For green rice, simply mix 2 cups cooked rice with ¼ cup of minced parsley.

Even if you don't want to attempt the "ducks"—a creation of the chef of the Singapura Inter Continental—you might serve fresh pineapple, diced or sliced to accompany this chicken dish.

STEAMBOAT

Serves 6

4 ounces lamb kidney, thinly sliced
4 ounces boneless steak, thinly sliced
4 ounces chicken breast meat, thinly sliced
4 ounces pork loin, thinly sliced
4 ounces red snapper fillet, cut into 1-inch strips
4 ounces shelled, cleaned shrimp, cut in half
2 ounces (about 1½ cups) spinach leaves, cut into 2-inch strips
2 ounces Chinese celery cut into 1-inch pieces (about 1 cup)
3 ounces (about 2 dozen) snow pea pods
1 bunch scallions, cut into 1-inch sections
6 eggs
3 cups beef broth
3 cups chicken broth

Have any or all of the above foods arranged in an attractive pattern on a Fresh-N-Fancy. Cover and refrigerate until ready to use. About 30 minutes before eating start steamboat. (See photo p. 83.) Rub the kettle with freshly grated ginger and pour hot chicken and beef broth into it to two-thirds capacity. Bring the broths to a boil before bringing to the dining room. Each person sits around the steamboat and places bits of food into the broth in front of him. As meal progresses broth becomes richer; it is consumed at end of meal. Serve with soy, sweet and sour sauce, hot mustard. Electric skillet may be substituted for steamboat.

Of course, you may vary the Steamboat ingredients to suit your taste. If you don't like kidney, substitute liver or omit entirely, for example.

Tasty and beautiful—Chicken Singapura.

SNACKS

Singapore has perfected outdoor eating snackery. Dozens of little stalls line the streets surrounded by "gossip stools." Here people like to congregate after work. Find the street that has the kind of food you prefer. In Bonhan Street try Chawabi, an Indian dish of fried prawn. At another stall, order an entire curry meal. On Beach Road, there are Malay dishes. Koek Road, Albert Street and People's Park specialize in Chinese food.

FRIED SPRING ROLLS

Makes 2 dozen

1 cup minced leeks (2 small leeks)
1 cup minced white turnip (2 small turnips)
½ cup minced carrot (1 large carrot)
¼ cup (2 ounces) bamboo shoots
4 ounces shredded crabmeat
4 ounces minced chicken meat
4 ounces cleaned, shelled, minced shrimp
¼ cup oil
1 teaspoon sherry
½ teaspoon monosodium glutamate
½ teaspoon sugar
½ teaspoon cornstarch
2 dozen spring roll skins
1 egg lightly beaten
oil for frying

Combine vegetables and meat; sauté quickly in oil, keeping the vegetables crisp. Add sherry, monosodium glutamate, sugar and cornstarch; stir to combine thoroughly. Cook 1 more minute. Place in sieve to remove any excess liquid. Cool before filling skins. Place 2 tablespoons filling on each skin; roll up from one corner, tucking in sides as you roll. Seal the opposite point, sealing with beaten egg. Fry the rolls two or three at a time in deep, moderately hot (350°F.) fat until golden, about 3 minutes. Drain on paper towels. Serve with sweet and sour sauce if desired. May be frozen in Cold Cut Keeper.

SPRING ROLL SKINS

1 egg, lightly beaten
2 cups flour
1 teaspoon salt
½ cup very cold water

Set aside one teaspoon of egg for sealing rolls. Combine remaining egg and other ingredients to make a dough. Cover and let rest 10 minutes. Turn out onto lightly floured Pastry Sheet. Knead until smooth and elastic. Divide dough into 16 pieces. Roll each into a 6-inch square—dough should be very thin. Fill as directed. (It is also possible to purchase these skins already made at Chinese grocery stores.)

A Singapore-style snack: Fried Spring Rolls.

It's worth the trip to Taipei to sample authentic Chinese cooking. Our Chinese restaurants are good, but they serve nothing to compare to the Cantonese and peppery Szechuan food that you'll eat in Taipei. Besides food, Taipei gives you the opportunity to see some of the Chinese culture that has been transplanted from the mainland. There's a new museum, several interesting Temples and performances of Chinese opera. Countryside and nearby mountains are lovely to see.

PICNICS

Mongolian Barbecue is unique to Taipei, but an idea with adaptations that can easily become one of your favorite ways of entertaining on your terrace or on a picnic. Once you've gotten past slicing the meats and vegetables, the rest of the preparation is easy. Guests select their own bowls of food, then the man of the house takes over the actual cooking at the grill.

Above: A typical, beautifully arranged Taipei snack.

MONGOLIAN BARBECUE

MEATS, sliced paper thin:

beef
pork
mutton
venison

SHREDDED VEGETABLES:

cabbage
green onions
green pepper
lettuce

LIQUIDS:

soy sauce (approximately 1 tablespoon)
sesame oil (approximately ½ teaspoon)
Din-Ding (hot salad oil) or hot pepper sauce (dash)
cooking wine (approximately 1 tablespoon)

Prepare a long buffet with meats, vegetables, cooking oils and condiments arranged in individual Cereal Bowls and Wonderliers. Give each guest a bowl and let him choose a few morsels from each of the three categories. It takes a little experimenting to come up with the seasoning you prefer, but this is part of the fun. In Taipei, the chef empties the bowl onto the top of the convex grill and cooks quickly, stirring with extra long chopsticks. There is a home-type Mongolian Barbecue available in this country, but you can approximate the taste by using a skillet over your barbecue or by cooking quickly on an electric skillet. Serve with hot sesame rolls, steaming tea.

PARTIES

After a delicious Chinese dinner, what would make an interesting dessert? Please avoid the inevitable canned pineapple! One idea is a fruit plate that consists of fresh pineapple, kumquats and canned lichee nuts — especially pleasing when served on a bed of crushed ice. Another impressive Chinese dessert that you can eat in both Hong Kong and Taipei is Glazed Bananas. It's delicious after Chinese food or any light entrée.

GLAZED BANANAS

Serves 4

4 bananas
¾ cup flour
1 egg, slightly beaten
½ cup water
3 cups peanut oil
½ cup sugar
½ teaspoon sesame seeds
1 teaspoon sesame oil

Peel bananas and cut into 1½ inch lengths. Coat with 1 tablespoon of the flour. Combine egg and remaining flour, beat well. Add ½ cup water and stir until batter is smooth. Coat bananas with batter. Heat peanut oil until it is very hot (400°F.), remove from heat. Add banana pieces one at a time to oil. When all have been added, return to heat and cook until the bananas are light brown. Drain the oil and set bananas aside. Combine remaining water and sugar in pan; cook, stirring occasionally, until sugar is dissolved. Add the sesame seeds and stir until mixture is thick and syrupy; add the oil and then the bananas. Stir and cook for about 1 minute. Pour out onto an oiled serving platter so that syrup as it cools and hardens will not stick to platter. A small bowl of cold water is served with this dish. The diner picks up a piece of banana, dips it into cold water to harden glaze before eating it.

Sweet but good. These collapse if left too long—try not to leave them longer than an hour. They're actually best if served as soon as cooked. Remember these, also, as a new side dish to serve with meat.

LOBSTER CURRY, LOBSTER PLAIN

Serves 2

2 live lobsters, about 1½ pounds each
1 egg white, slightly beaten
2 teaspoons cornstarch
3 tablespoons lard or cooking oil

SEASONING PLAIN

1 tablespoon lard or cooking oil
2 slices fresh ginger
¼ cup bamboo shoots, well drained
1 carrot, thinly sliced
6 small pieces broccoli, trimmed
1 teaspoon cornstarch
2 teaspoons Saki
¼ cup water
½ teaspoon salt

SEASONING CURRY

1 tablespoon lard or cooking oil
1 scallion, minced
2 teaspoons sugar
1 teaspoon cornstarch
1 tablespoon water
2 teaspoons curry powder
2 teaspoons Saki
empty lobster shell, boiled 20 minutes

Wash lobster, cut spinal cord by inserting a knife where the tail and body meet. Turn on back and split lengthwise. Remove and discard the dark vein, the sac near the head, and spongy tissue, but save green liver and coral, if any. Remove all meat from body and claws and slice pieces on diagonal. Combine beaten egg white and cornstarch in 3-cup Wonderlier. Add cut up lobster and stir into cornstarch mixture. Allow to marinate in

Ready to cook: Mongolian Barbecue ingredients

The chef at work cooking Mongolian Barbecue.

Delicious party dessert—Glazed Bananas.

this at least 3 hours in refrigerator. Heat 3 tablespoons lard in frypan. Add marinated meat. Fry over high heat about 3 minutes, or until lightly browned. Remove and set aside. Heat the 1 tablespoon lard for Seasoning Plain in frypan. Add vegetables and sauté over high heat about 3 minutes. Combine water with cornstarch to make a smooth paste. Add, with remaining ingredients and ½ the browned lobster pieces, to vegetables. Simmer 6 minutes over low heat, or until lobster is tender. In a second frypan heat 1 tablespoon lard for Seasoning Curry. Add scallion and sauté over high heat 1 minute. Combine sugar and cornstarch, add water to make a smooth paste. Add with remaining ingredients to scallion in pan. Add remaining lobster meat and simmer about 6 minutes, or until lobster is tender. Serve lobster plain on one side of large oval platter and lobster curry on other side. Place boiled, empty lobster shell across center, dividing two lobster mixtures.

SNACKS

In the Orient, food presentation is an art. Nothing is served haphazardly. Components of typical Chinese snack meal are simple enough: Chinese mushrooms, ham, chicken, duck, goose, red and green peppers. The beauty of the arrangement, however, makes the food truly impressive. Try serving our Roast Chicken prettily: perhaps on small lacquer trays. Garnish the chicken Taipei-style with kumquats and bananas.

ROAST CHICKEN, CANTONESE STYLE

Serves 3 to 4

1 3½-pound roasting chicken
1 tablespoon salt
¼ teaspoon cinnamon
¼ teaspoon black pepper
1 tablespoon molasses
2 tablespoons boiling water
peanut oil

Immerse the chicken in boiling water for 2 minutes. Combine salt, cinnamon and black pepper, roast in 350°F. oven 5 minutes. Rub roasted salt inside chicken. Dilute the molasses with boiling water and rub over surface of chicken. Hang to dry for 4 hours, or place on a rack and allow to dry thoroughly. Heat enough oil to cover chicken to 350°F. Fry chicken 20 to 25 minutes or until outside is golden and meat is done. Cut into small pieces, cutting through bone, to serve.

An eight-hour flight from Honolulu will put you in fascinating Tokyo. On the surface, you'll find a Westernized city. Its dress, modern skyscrapers and crowded shopping district — the Ginza —are like our own. Delve deeper to find the traditional Japan. Stay at least one night at a Ryokan, a Japanese Inn. Go to see a performance of Kabuki or Noh drama, Japan's traditional forms of theatre. Marvel at the exquisite simplicity of Japan's gardens, and at its tea ceremony.

PICNICS

The food sections of department stores and specialty markets are phenomenal. Aisle after aisle has fascinating, strange-to-us delicacies, the food beautifully arranged in displays or in wooden boxes. Ask for an interpreter to guide you in your selections for a picnic. Yakitori is the Japanese way of barbecuing skewered meats—a most delicious thought for a picnic.

YAKITORI

Serves 4 to 6

¼ pound duck meat, cut into 1-inch pieces
1½ green peppers, split, seeded, parboiled
¼ pound ground chicken balls (see below)
¼ pound chicken livers, quartered
¼ pound (2 or 3) chicken wings, cut at joints
¼ pound gizzards, skinned and cut into ½-inch pieces
¼ pound chicken meat, cut into 1-inch pieces

Above: Even a picnic, Japanese-style, is beautiful and artistically arranged.

¼ cup soy

¼ cup Mirin (sweet Saki)

2 tablespoons sugar

Broil duck meat 5 minutes or until slightly brown. Cut peppers in eighths to form pieces large enough to wrap around duck meat cubes. Wrap each duck cube with a piece of green pepper, set aside. Ask butcher to grind ¼ pound chicken meat or grind it yourself. Form into balls with a 1-inch diameter. Prepare skewers alternating the various fowl. Combine soy, Mirin and sugar, simmer over moderate heat until sugar dissolves. Brush on skewers. Broil skewers 10 minutes or until fowl is cooked. Brush with sauce as meats broil. Carry meats to picnic in separate Square Rounds.

PARTIES

Unlike many countries where it is almost impossible to find "native" food, Tokyo abounds in Japanese restaurants. Most specialize in a specific dish. Try Sukiyaki, Tempura, Mitzutaki and Teppan-yaki, the current Tokyo eating vogue. All four are party dishes where time-consuming preparation is done ahead. Cooking can be done quickly at the table with utensils you buy there or with tabletop American appliances.

TEPPAN–YAKI

Serves 4

1 pound boneless steak, thinly sliced

2 large potatoes, sliced ¼ inch thick

2 large onions, thinly sliced

3 bell peppers, stems and seeds removed, sliced in half vertically

2 mushrooms, sliced vertically

½ pound fresh spinach leaves

4 tablespoons oil

4 tablespoons butter

⅛ teaspoon minced garlic

barbecue sauce

½ cup Mitzutaki Sauce (see Mitzutaki recipe)

Place steak and vegetables in Pie Taker in an attractive pattern. Blend butter and garlic and place in Sauce Dish, set aside until cooking time. When guests are assembled, each may choose the amount of meat and vegetable desired. Heat oil in large skillet and sauté all ingredients. First cook potatoes and peppers 5 minutes, then add remaining ingredients and cook all until vegetables are tender and meat brown. Serve garlic butter, barbecue sauce or Mitzutaki Sauce, or all three, and allow guests to spread on their own portions.

This was especially good with the garlic butter and the Mitzutaki Sauce. The barbecue sauce makes it more like a standard meal we are used to. This could all be packed in the Pie Taker and taken to a picnic. The food would be cooked on a griddle over a camp fire—easy to do.

SUKIYAKI OKURA

Serves 4

1 pound boneless steak, thinly sliced

1 bunch leeks (about 8) cut into 1-inch julienne

3 yellow onions, sliced

16 to 20 mushrooms, sliced

½ pound Tofu (bean curd) cut into ½-inch cubes

1 pound Shirataki (Japanese vermicelli noodles)

1 bunch watercress

1 cup Mirin (sweet Saki)

½ cup Shoyu (Japanese soy sauce)

¼ cup sugar

4 eggs

Arrange the vegetables and meat in Pie Taker, overlapping the slices of beef and grouping the vegetables in an interesting pattern. Combine mirin, shoyu and sugar in medium Mixing Bowl. Rub a piece of beef fat on large electric skillet until pan is well greased. Place slices of beef in skillet and turn as soon as they change color. Push meat to one side of pan. Add onions, leeks, mushrooms and bean curd. Add Mirin liquid and simmer 10 minutes, turning occasionally. Add watercress. When watercress wilts, sukiyaki is ready. Each person breaks a raw egg into a small bowl and helps himself from the skillet, placing his portion on a plate, then dips a hot morsel into the beaten egg to cool it. Serve with rice and tea.

MITZUTAKI

Serves 4

SAUCE

½ cup Mirin (sweet Saki)

½ cup soy sauce

¼ cup lemon juice

¼ cup vinegar

¼ cup seaweed

MAIN DISH

3 cups beef bouillon

3 cups water

1 pound boneless steak, very thinly sliced

½ pound Chinese cabbage, cut into 1-inch sections

½ pound Tofu (bean curd) cut into 1-inch blocks

½ pound rice noodles

2 onions, thinly sliced

1 cup crysanthemum leaves (picked from garden when available)

chopped scallions

grated horseradish

Combine sauce ingredients in a 2-cup Square Round; let stand for 2 hours. Drain off seaweed and use as a dip for mitzutaki. This should be made at table, with guests cooking their own food in the boiling bouillon. Pour bouillon and water into electric frypan or chafing dish. Arrange meats and vegetables in attractive pattern in Pie Taker and bring to table. Guests dip food into broth until cooked. Food is then put on own plate and dipped into Mirin mixture. Scallions and horse radish are served with this. When everyone is finished cooking, the broth is served as a soup.

TEMPURA

Serves 6

½ pound large fresh shrimp, shelled and deveined

6 whitebait or fresh sardines

1 pound eel, boned and cut into pieces (or substitute scallops)

1 package (10 ounces) frozen lobster tails

10 mushrooms, halved

½ small eggplant, cut in 2 x ½-inch strips

½ pound sweet potatoes, pared and sliced ⅛-inch thick

2 large green peppers, cut lengthwise in ¼-inch slices

salad oil

Batter (recipe below)

Drop shrimp into boiling, salted

water to cover; return to boil. Reduce heat; simmer, covered, for 5 minutes, drain and cool. Drop whitebait into boiling salted water to cover, bring back to boil and remove. Drop eel into boiling, salted water to cover, return to boil. Reduce heat; simmer covered 5 minutes, remove. Cook lobster tails as package directs. Drain, cool and shell, halve meat crosswise. In Pie Taker arrange meats and vegetables in an attractive pattern. Refrigerate, covered, until ready to cook Tempura.

BATTER

3 eggs
2½ teaspoons soy sauce
1⅔ cups flour
2 tablespoons sugar
1 teaspoon salt

Make batter just before using. Beat eggs with rotary beater; add soy and 1¼ cups water. Gradually add flour, sugar and salt, beating until smooth. Makes 2⅓ cups.

SAUCE

½ cup Mirin (sweet Saki)
½ cup beef bouillon
1 cup soy
horseradish, freshly grated
ginger root, freshly grated

In small saucepan combine Mirin, bouillon and soy, bring to boil; pour into 6 individual Sauce Dishes. Cook Tempura at table in electric skillet or deep fryer. Fill skillet with oil to depth of 3 inches, heat to moderate (350°). With tongs, dip fish and vegetables into batter to coat lightly. Deep-fry a few pieces at a time until lightly browned, about 3 minutes. Serve with sauce, allowing each guest to add horseradish or ginger to his own.

SNACKS

Sushi snack bars are everywhere. Around lunchtime, little stands are set up outside. People dash up, buy a few sushi and rush back to their offices. Sushi is seaweed-wrapped rice with a variety of fillings—don't be reluctant to try! Onigiri is another favorite and a lesson in how to be imaginative with rice. Hot rice is filled with tidbits to give flavor contrast to the blandness. The rice is then molded into decorative shapes.

Ready to cook quickly and serve: Teppan-yaki

To be quickly cooked—and eaten—Tempura.

ONIGIRI (RICE BALLS)

1 dozen

3 cups rice (about 1½ pounds)
3½ cups water
1½ sheets nori (seaweed)
2 ounces smoked salmon
¼ cup red caviar
2 pickled plums or peaches

Bring water to a boil in large saucepan. Add rice; when water comes back to a boil lower heat, simmer 15 minutes. Turn heat off and keep lid on 5 to 6 minutes. Wet hands and sprinkle with salt. Take nori and cut to fit Pie Wedges. Place a piece on bottom of each of 12 Pie Wedges. Top with ⅓ cup rice and firmly press to fit wedge shape. Place smoked salmon on top of 4 wedges, ½ a plum or peach on another 4 and 1 tablespoon caviar on each of remaining 4 wedges. Cover with remaining rice. Press firmly to obtain wedge shape and stick rice firmly together. Top with remaining nori triangles. Cover and store until ready to eat.

SUSHI

Serves 6 to 8

FILLING I

2 eggs
4 teaspoons Saki
1 tablespoon sugar
½ teaspoon salt

¼ cup oil
3 ounces fillet of sole
flour
¼ pound spinach, cleaned and cooked (½ cup cooked)

Mix eggs with wine, sugar and salt. Heat 2 tablespoons oil in small frypan. Add eggs and scramble; remove from heat and set aside. Cut fish into long strips about ¼ inch wide, dust with flour. Add remaining oil to frypan and sauté fish until it flakes, about 3 to 4 minutes. Place with spinach and eggs in Cereal Bowl and set aside until ready to finish Sushi.

CHEESE FILLING

1¼ pounds Cheddar cheese
2 canned green chilies, cut in thin strips

Cut ½-inch thick slices of cheese into triangles, with each side about 2 inches long. Place on the pastry round with a strip of green chili.

The dough is very elastic and easy to work with, very flaky when fried. Fillings can be frozen in Square Rounds.

FILLING II

3 ounces (about 6) shrimp, shelled and deveined
2 eggs
2 tablespoons Saki
1 tablespoon sugar
¼ teaspoon salt
2 tablespoons oil

Chop shrimp very fine; blend with eggs, wine, sugar and salt. Heat oil in frypan, add eggs and cook, stirring constantly, until shrimp are done, about 3 to 4 minutes. Set aside.

RICE

2½ cups water
½ cup white vinegar
1 tablespoon sugar
1 teaspoon salt
2 cups rice
2 sheets seaweed

Bring water, vinegar, sugar and salt to a boil, add rice and return to the boil. Simmer, covered, 15 minutes. Turn heat off and keep lid on 5 to 6 minutes. Place seaweed in warm water for 2 to 3 minutes to soften. Place 1 sheet, about 10 x 6, on a bamboo lattice or a clean kitchen towel. Place half of rice on seaweed and spread evenly, leaving about 1¼-inch border of seaweed. Place ½ of either filling down center of rice (if using Filling I, place ingredients one on top of the other to form tri-colored center). Roll up like a jelly roll, keeping ingredients carefully in at both ends so that seaweed encases all ingredients. Roll to a perfect cylinder, leaving a margin of seaweed to overlap. It is important to roll rice while quite warm to insure its sticking. Use cloth to push the roll into shape. When rolled, remove cloth and slice into eight sections. Repeat procedure with remaining rice, filling. Store in Bread Server or Cold Cut Keeper.

These are impossible to stop eating. The eggs with the Saki are wonderful and a perfect combination with the vinegar rice. Be sure to use the lacy seaweed, not the dashi konbu, which is merely used as a soup flavoring.

san juan

San Juan, the capital city of Puerto Rico, founded in 1521 by the Spaniards, now reigns as a gay vacationland. To see San Juan as it was before the luxury hotels took over, visit the old part of the city. The many fine examples of Spanish colonial architecture, with wrought iron grills, balconies and interior patios, give you a taste of Old San Juan. If you possibly can, visit other parts of the island, too, lush mountains or another coastal area to find still-unspoiled havens.

PICNICS

Picnic in the mountains or at the beach, but be sure to pack a lunch for one of your excursions. The scenery is so relaxing you'll want to enjoy it at leisure. At Las Croabas, rent a sloop for the day, sail to a deserted island, swim, snorkel and picnic. Our recipe here is meant for patio entertaining. Pineapple Bombay is a Caribbean version of seafood curry —a particularly delicious one.

Above: A Puerto Rican picnic at Las Croabas.

PINEAPPLE BOMBAY

Serves 6

1 apple, cored and diced
1 onion, diced
2 stalks celery, cut in pieces
½ cup butter
½ cup flour
¼ cup chutney, cut in small pieces
2 teaspoons curry powder
1 quart chicken broth, heated
2 pounds assorted seafood (shrimps, scallops, lobster)
¼ cup sherry

½ cup heavy cream
3 medium-sized pineapples
2 fried bananas, trisected and each section split
almonds
coconut chips

Sauté apple, onion and celery in 6 tablespoons butter until tender. Add the flour, chutney and curry powder; cook over low heat, stirring constantly for 3 or 4 minutes. Add heated broth, a little at a time, beating constantly. Simmer 10 minutes. Strain sauce and set aside. Melt remaining butter and sauté seafood 4 minutes, stirring constantly. Add sherry and combine with curry sauce; simmer 10 minutes. Remove from heat and add cream. Split pineapples lengthwise, being careful to retain some leaves with each half. Scoop out fruit. Wrap leaves with foil and place pineapple shells in large roasting pan. Put in moderate oven until heated, about 10 minutes. Fill with seafood mixture and return to oven for 5 minutes. Decorate pineapple with bananas, sprinkle with almonds and coconut. Serve with rice if desired.

PARTIES

Guitar cake is a spectacular party dessert. It is time-consuming but not difficult. An easier version uses a Party Susan and copies part of the fruit design. Guests help themselves to a "slice" of the fruit and the pudding underneath. Another unusual centerpiece idea from Puerto Rico: use raw ingredients for paella as focal point on an hors d'oeuvre buffet. Half hour before eating, remove paella to kitchen for cooking.

BANJO PUDDING DESSERT

Serves 10 to 12

3 packages cooked or instant pudding, any flavor
1 cup (8¾-ounce can) peach halves
1 cup (8¾-ounce can) pear halves
1 cup (8¾-ounce can) apricot halves
17 pitted bing cherries
1 slice canned pineapple
2 bananas, split lengthwise
shredded coconut
½ cup apricot preserves
2 tablespoons sugar

Prepare puddings according to package directions. Pour into Party Susan, distributing equally among sections. Let set. Drain fruits and dry well. Place banana halves around outside edges of 4 of the 6 sections of Party Susan. Line remaining outer edges with 11 cherries – this will be the top of the circle. Fill center ring with pineapple slice, top with a peach half. Place apricot halves attractively along banana-section edges. Slice remaining peaches and pears into 5 slices each. Place 5 slices of pear, overlapping each other, in one section of Party Susan, with centers touching pineapple ring. Do this in three alternate sections, fill remaining three sections in like manner with peach slices. Place 1 of the remaining cherries at each place where banana ends meet. Place remaining cherries on top of apricot halves. Fill in open spaces with coconut in an attractive design. Melt preserves with sugar; strain and spread over fruit. Chill until ready to serve.

GUITAR CAKE

Serves 16

1 1-pound can apricot halves
1 1-pound can pitted dark sweet cherries, drained
1 1-pound can peach halves, drained
1 1-pound can pear halves, drained
1 14-ounce can guava shells, drained
½ cup Curaçao
1 pineapple ring
2 packages yellow cake mix
4 or 5 small bananas
lemon juice
1 cup apricot preserves
1 4-ounce can (1½ cups) shredded coconut

Drain apricot halves and reserve ¼ cup syrup. Combine apricots, cherries, peaches, pears, guava shells and pineapple ring in 2-quart wonderlier. Combine reserved apricot syrup and Curaçao and pour over fruit. Marinate overnight. Prepare cake mixes according to package directions. Pour into 3 layer-cake pans—a 10" round, 8" round, and 8" square. Bake according to package directions and cool. Cut ¼"-slice from top of each circle so that 2 circles make flat edge when they meet. Put together to form body of guitar. Cut a 2" x 8" strip from 8" square cake. Place at top end of 8" round to form neck of guitar. Place cake on a large board at least 28" long and 16" wide. Drain marinated fruits thoroughly. Peel and slice bananas in half lengthwise and brush with lemon juice to prevent browning. Place bananas cut side down along outer edges of guitar, forming a banana rim. Place apricot halves at bottom of guitar, overlapping closely. Place an overlapping row of guava shells just above row of apricots. Place pineapple ring in center of guitar at point where 8" and 10" circles meet. Cover with 1 peach half. Slice remaining peaches and pears into 24 thin slices each and place as spokes around pineapple—grouping 6 slices of pear, then 6 slices of peach and alternating around the pineapple. Make an arch above top part of spoke with cherries and fill in remaining cake with guava shells. Place cherries at each connecting point of banana slices and anywhere else they seem appropriate. Melt apricot preserves over low heat and use to glaze fruits. Brush sides of guitar with glaze and cover with grated coconut.

A chef's masterpiece: delicious Guitar Cake.

WILLEMSTAD

Curaçao has everything—a wonderful climate, a distinct foreign flavor, good beaches, and marvelous food. Dishes such as Kapucijners, and traditions such as a hearty breakfast, can be traced to Curaçao's strong ties with Holland. The picturesque harbor area in Willemstad, de Ruyterkade Street, is in fact named after its Amsterdam counterpart. The restaurants and hotels feature the gamut of international cusine. And—not to be missed—are many excellent dishes native to Curaçao.

PICNICS

Curaçao beaches are pleasantly uncrowded. Picnic on local specialties such as Kesita and Hajaccas. At East Point, people fish for a picnic lunch of sea urchins. (Bring a friend who has the equipment and know-how.) After their spines are clipped, the urchins are halved. They must be instantly chilled — drop in an ice cube, douse with lemon, spoon out a delicacy.

HAJACCAS

Serves 10

FILLING

1½ pounds pork, cooked and cut into ½-inch cubes
1½ pounds ham, cut into ½-inch cubes
½ pound boned chicken cut into ½-inch pieces
2 large tomatoes, peeled and cut in small pieces
3 large onions, chopped
2 large cloves garlic, minced
1 red pepper, cut in small pieces
1 green pepper, cut in small pieces
1 cup beef broth
½ cup raisins
½ cup almonds, blanched
¼ pound butter
¼ cup capers
20 pitted prunes
10 black olives, pitted
1½ teaspoons salt

Red snapper: colorful when caught, even more so when prepared Curaçao style.

MANSA

2½ cups corn meal
1 teaspoon salt
gravy from filling

Combine filling ingredients in large saucepan, simmer 10 minutes or until vegetables are tender, set aside. Mix corn meal with gravy (about 1 cup) until it makes a paste. Cut heavy foil to rectangles 10 x 8 inches. Place 3 tablespoons paste on each rectangle, spread out with a wet knife down center of foil. Put filling mixture on top, making sure a piece of ham, olive, capers and prune is in each. Fold foil like an envelope and place in a large saucepan. Cover with boiling water, simmer 2 hours.

An excellent picnic "meal in one" idea, these can be packed in the Cold Cut Keeper. The filling can be made well in advance and the Mansa just before cooking. Filling fits in 2-quart Wonderlier.

KESITA

2½ dozen

6 egg whites (about 1 cup)
1 pound grated Cheddar cheese
2 teaspoons red pepper
fat for frying

Beat egg whites until foamy. Add cheese and pepper; continue beating until mixture stands in soft peaks. Drop by tablespoonfuls into hot (400°F.) fat until kesita are golden. Drain and serve.

Very good Cheddar-flavored appetizer, almost like a light, lacy fritter. Good cold as well as warm.

PARTIES

Keshy Yena is a party dish that can make your reputation as a hostess. The dish can be made in two versions, one with fish, the other—which we've chosen—an elaborate, delicious splurge using meat and a whole Edam. Next are two interesting party suggestions utilizing food abundant on the island. The red snapper is one of the Caribbean's most popular fishes. Sopito is an unusual chowder-type soup, with coconut and cod.

KESHY YENA CURACAO INTER CONTINENTAL

Serves 20

4 pounds round, cut in thin strips
½ cup flour
1½ cups butter
½ cup brandy
5 red peppers, seeded, cut in ½-inch squares
3 green peppers, seeded, cut in ½-inch squares

Picnic elegantly in Curaçao on the beach at Santa Barbara.

3 large onions, minced
1 pound mushrooms, sliced
5 hard-cooked eggs, peeled, chopped
1¼ cups raisins
1¼ cups pitted ripe olives, sliced
1¼ cups chopped pickles
¼ cup ketchup
3 cans (10½-ounce) golden mushroom soup
1 4-pound Edam cheese

Dry beef well, sprinkle with flour, mix to coat thoroughly. Melt 1 cup butter in large frypan. Sauté meat until brown on all sides. If necessary, do in 2 or 3 batches to give meat enough room to brown. When meat is brown, pour warm brandy over it and flambé. When flambé dies down, remove meat and liquid, set aside. Melt remaining butter in frypan. Add peppers, onions and mushrooms, sauté until lightly brown. Add eggs, raisins, olives, pickles, ketchup and meat. Simmer, stirring occasionally, until meat is tender, about 15 minutes. Remove from heat. Drain liquid and reserve. Put meat mixture in Fix-N-Mix. Return liquid to pan and reduce to 1 cup. Combine with soup, blending until smooth. Add to meat mixture, stir until well blended. Set aside until ready to finish casserole. Line a 6-quart or 2 3-quart casseroles with ¼-inch slices of cheese with rind removed. Pour meat mixture into casserole and cover with remaining cheese slices. Bake in 350°F. oven 15 minutes or until cheese is melted and casserole bubbly.

Very unusual, tasty casserole. Flavors all blend to a mild meat au gratin and outside shell is chewy and fun to eat.

Keshy Yena has a delicious crust of Edam cheese.

CALA

84 appetizers

¼ pound (½ cup) black-eyed beans
1½ red or green bell peppers
1 teaspoon salt
oil

Soak beans overnight in water. Drain and remove skins. Grind beans, peppers and salt together in food mill or place in blender. Beat until mixture is fluffy. Pour oil into skillet to depth of 1 inch. Heat until a drop of bean mixture sizzles as it touches the oil. Drop bean mixture by teaspoonfuls into the hot oil. Fry until golden on one side, turn and fry on other side. Drain on paper and serve hot. Mixture may be prepared several days in advance of cooking, stored in 16-ounce Square Round.

RED SNAPPER

Serves 2 to 3

1 onion, chopped (½ cup)
1 green pepper, chopped
2 tablespoons cooking oil
2 tomatoes, chopped
1 teaspoon tomato paste

1 small clove garlic, minced
1 pound red snapper fillet
3 tablespoons butter

Sauté onion and green pepper in oil until tender. Add tomatoes, tomato paste and garlic. Cover and simmer ½ hour. Sauté snapper in butter 5 minutes or until fish begins to flake. Add sauce and simmer 5 minutes more.

A very colorful, flavorful recipe, one of the best for fish fillet I have seen.

SOPITO

6 Cups

1 coconut
1 cup boiling water
1 pound salt pork
1 onion, minced
1 tomato, minced
⅛ teaspoon red pepper
1 pound cod, cut in 1-inch cubes
3 tablespoons flour
1 tablespoon butter
1 quart water
¼ cup lemon juice
grated nutmeg

Open coconut and reserve milk. Shred meat and soak in boiling water 15 minutes; squeeze through cheesecloth. Put reserved coconut milk and coconut extract into large saucepan. Add meat, simmer 30 minutes. Add onion, tomato and red pepper, simmer 45 minutes or until meat is tender. Add fish and cook another 10 minutes, or until fish flakes. Knead flour with butter, stir into fish mixture; blend thoroughly. Add remaining water and lemon juice, simmer 10 minutes. Serve with a sprinkle of nutmeg and a slice of lemon.

SNACKS

Curaçao has some of the best shopping in the world, with shops filled with intriguing wares. At the harbor, you can buy fresh fruit from the boats that come over from Venezuela. Visit art galleries featuring the work of local artists and the museum with antiques from the old Dutch estate houses. After a long, busy day, it's time to stop for a late-afternoon snack, a cooling fruit punch, a taste of Curaçao's varied hors d'oeuvres.

PASTECHI

Makes 48

2 tablespoons minced onion
2 tablespoons minced leek
2 cloves garlic, finely chopped
½ teaspoon salt
¼ teaspoon ground pepper
2 tablespoons butter
¾ pound shrimp peeled, deveined and cut into small pieces
pastry for 2 2-crust pies

Sauté onion, leek, garlic, salt and pepper in butter until soft but not brown. Add shrimp and sauté until pink. Roll out pastry and cut into 2-inch circles. Moisten edges of pastry and fold in half. Seal edges firmly. Fry in hot oil (400°F.) about 3 minutes or until pastry is golden. Serve at once. If desired, pastechi may be fried 1 minute, cooled and frozen on cookie sheet. When hard they should be stored in a Snack-Stor. They can be fried frozen at 400° for 2 minutes before serving.

Delicious—flaky outside crust an excellent contrast to shrimp.

Roundup, South American style—exciting prelude to a parrillada.

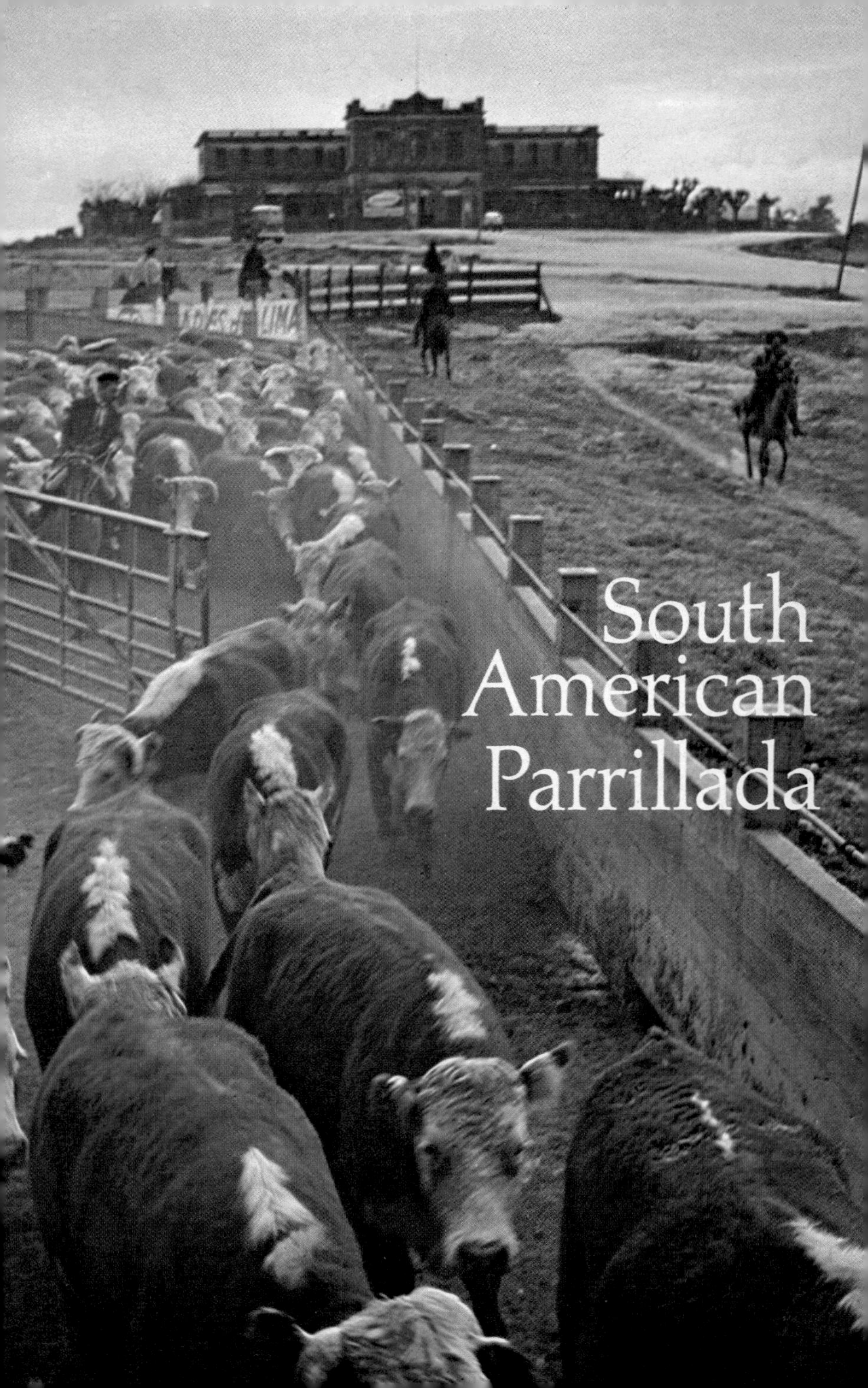

South American Parrillada

South American Spit Roast or Asado Criollo produces the most succulent beef in the world.

Parrillada (in Brazil, Argentina and Uruguay, particularly) is the term applied to the ingredients of an asado (roast) but you'll often find the terms Asado Criollo and Parrillada used interchangeably. It's easier to remember that any meat designated as a "la parrilla" will mean that it has been broiled over charcoal.

The method of cooking is fascinating. Our picture shows how Parrillada is prepared at Churrascaria Gaucho in Rio. A huge pit is dug in the ground and filled with charcoal. All types of meat, from whole sides of beef to sausage, are impaled on huge skewers placed vertically around the fire.

The method is slow roasting for one to two hours or more. Meat is first cleaned and trimmed so there is little fat, and it is washed in salt and water. The meat is turned during cooking so it roasts evenly. When done, it is moved away from the fire to keep warm without further cooking. Usually three kinds of meat are served as part of a parrillada, in this order: sausages, giblets and assorted meats.

Parrillada Uruguaya would consist of grilled beef tenderloin, veal, pork chops, lamb chops, bacon, kidney, sausages and tomatoes served on a bed of burning charcoal. You can see why, with meat-eating habits like this, the Uruguayans must refrain from eating meat three times a week — Friday, Saturday and Sunday — so some meat will be left for export.

La Tablada, a typical ranch just outside Montevideo, is worth an early — 7 a.m. — visit to watch an authentic gaucho roundup. Cattle and sheep are weighed and sold. When the gauchos' work is over, they retire to the main building of the ranch to relax, get their hair cut, play pool, drink maté (a strong green tea made of the leaf of a kind of holly) and eat freshly barbecued steak for breakfast.

As accompaniments to Parrillada you may eat Farofa (manioc meal) and a salad. The salad usually served consists of lettuce, tomatoes, onions, cucumbers, and hearts of palm, with a vinaigrette dressing. Chopped tomatoes and onions are also served — use these on top of the meats as a relish.

It is possible to approximate a parrillada at home on our regulation barbecue grills. Here is one recipe developed by La Fonda del Sol. You'll find other Parrillada recipes throughout our South America section.

GRILLED LATIN AMERICAN SAUSAGES

Serves 6

9 spicy chorizos (Spanish sausage)
9 mild chorizos
2 red peppers
2 green peppers

Cut peppers into squares (about 2-inches) alternate on skewer a piece of green pepper, mild sausage, red pepper and spicy sausage. Grill well on both sides. Serve with sauce.

SAUCE

Makes 6 cups

2 green peppers
2 red peppers
2 red onions, cut into julienne strips
4 tablespoons cooking oil
6 fresh, peeled and seeded tomatoes, cut into ¼-inch squares
4 shallots, minced
¼ teaspoon crushed red pepper
⅛ teaspoon oregano
⅛ teaspoon salt
⅛ teaspoon monosodium glutamate

Split and seed peppers, cut into julienne strips; sauté with onions in oil until crisp, not wilted. Add remaining ingredients, simmer 10 minutes. Serve over sausages.

A very colorful, tasty dish. The sauce is really more like a vegetable stew and can be a complete meal. The sauce could be prepared ahead and stored until ready to be reheated.

A typical in-the-ground barbecue pit.

TOSTADOS

(Filled Tortillas or Arepas – fillings on pp 130-131)

Makes 10

1¾ cups harina de maiz (cornmeal)
1¼ cups unsifted all purpose flour
1 teaspoon salt
3 tablespoons lard
¾ cup warm milk

Combine cornmeal, flour and salt in large bowl. Cut in shortening with pastry blender. Add warm milk (use more if necessary to make a dough), stirring until mixture is completely moistened. Form into a ball and turn out onto floured board. Work with hands until no longer sticky, about 5 minutes. Divide in half, place in 1-quart Wonderlier. Seal and let rest ½ hour. Roll out each ball on floured Sheet to make 18-inch circle. Cut five 5-inch tortillas from each circle. Bake on heated, ungreased griddle, 1 minute on each side.

Our first South American stop is the ultra-modern city of Caracas, Venezuela, a city with two postures. It is impressive as a thriving metropolis, thanks to its modernity, well-kept plazas and parks, and petroleum economy. On the other hand, Caracas has every right to be considered a resort target. There are mountains surrounding the city adding greatly to its physical charm, and just a half hour away is the seacoast with unspoiled beaches tourists always search out.

PICNICS

It's not that steak isn't delicious —it's just that food presented in the same old way year after year without embellishment becomes a bore. Venezuelan Carne Asado takes the barbecue steak out of its rut and gives it a new flavoring — a whole new lease on life. Overnight marinating guarantees that a less expensive cut of meat will be deliciously tender by barbecue time.

TAMANACO CARNE ASADO

Serves 4 to 6

½ cup chopped onion (1 medium onion)
¼ cup oil
¼ cup red wine
2 tomatoes, chopped
1 green pepper, seeded and chopped
2 teaspoons salt
½ teaspoon pepper
2 pounds top round steak, cut 1½ -inch thick

Combine first seven ingredients. Place steak in Cold Cut Keeper and cover with marinade; leave overnight, turning occasionally. Broil over hot coals, about 8 to 10 minutes on each side for medium rare. Brush with marinade as meat cooks. Heat any remaining marinade and use as a sauce over grilled meat.

This has excellent flavor, and meat is very tender because of the overnight marinating. Meat should be sliced thinly on the diagonal for best results.

PARTIES

The Piñata, a huge paper figure, originated in Venezuela and has been enthusiastically imported into this country. At a Piñata Party, the figure—usually a popular cartoon — is set upon with sticks until he spills forth trinkets. At your next children's party with or without Piñata, it would be fun to serve typical Piñata Party sweets. In a grown-up vein, try Pabellon Criollo, considered a workingman's meal but, to us, a very fine party dish.

PABELLON

Serves 8 to 10

3-pound chuck roast
½ cup water
1 beef bouillon cube
2 tablespoons cooking oil
1 medium onion, chopped
2 cloves garlic, minced
2 tomatoes, peeled, chopped

Place meat in saucepan, add water and bouillon cube. Cover and simmer gently until tender, about 2 hours. Halfway through cooking, check liquid and add more if needed — liquid should be completely evaporated when meat is done. Remove and cool. Pull apart so that meat is in long, thin shreds. Set aside. Heat oil in frypan, add onion and garlic, sauté until tender. Add tomatoes and shreds of meat. Simmer on very low heat 15 minutes. Serve with white rice and black beans.

WHITE RICE

2 tablespoons butter
1 cup white rice
1 onion, minced
2 cloves garlic, minced
2 cups water
¼ pimiento, sliced

Melt butter in saucepan. Add rice, onion and garlic; sauté over moderate heat, stirring constantly, until rice just starts to brown. Add water and pimiento. Cover and simmer about 20 minutes, or until rice is tender and water absorbed.

BLACK BEANS

1 pound black beans
3 tablespoons cooking oil
1 onion, minced
4 cloves garlic, minced
1 red pimiento, sliced
⅛ teaspoon cumin
4 fried eggs
3 fried plantains

Wash beans and place in 2-quart Wonderlier. Cover with water and let soak 2 hours. Heat oil in frypan, add vegetables and cumin, sauté until vegetables are tender. Set aside. Place beans in large kettle, cover with 6 cups water. Simmer 1 hour or until beans are tender, adding more water if necessary. Blend in cooked vegetables and salt to taste. Serve meat, rice and beans on one large platter. Garnish with eggs and plantain. Serve tostados on the side.

This is both attractive and delicious — all flavors blend very well. Pabellon can be prepared ahead and reheated just before serving. Both beans and rice should have 2 or 3 tablespoons water added to pot just before reheating.

BIENMESABE

Serves 10 to 12

4 cups coconut milk (recipe below)
¼ pound (1 stick) butter
5 tablespoons cornstarch
½ cup cold water
¾ cup sugar
8 egg yolks, lightly beaten
1 cup heavy cream, whipped
30 champagne biscuits

Combine coconut milk and butter in saucepan. Combine cornstarch and water to make a smooth paste, stir into hot milk. Add sugar, cook over low heat, stirring constantly, until sauce is thickened — about 10 minutes. Remove from heat. Stir 1 cup of the hot sauce into the beaten eggs, a little at a time, beating constantly. Return egg mixture to saucepan and cook over low heat, stirring constantly, 2 minutes, or until eggs thicken mixture slightly. Remove from heat, cover and cool thoroughly. Fold in whipped cream. Cover the bottom of a 2-quart Wonderlier with biscuits. Cover with part of the sauce, continue this process until all ingredients are used. Garnish with grated coconut if desired.

A smooth, strongly coconut-flavored sauce, rich and delicious—nice combination with the biscuits.

COCONUT MILK

From canned coconut:

1 4-ounce can (about 1⅓ cups) coconut
1⅓ cups milk

Combine milk and coconut in an electric blender; cover and blend at high speed about 40 seconds. Or combine coconut and milk in a saucepan and cook, stirring constantly, over low heat until mixture foams, about 2 minutes. Strain, pressing coconut to drain all liquid. Makes 1 cup liquid.

From a fresh coconut:

Crack open coconut; pare brown skin and grate coconut meat. Combine with 1⅓ cups fresh scalded milk. Let stand 20 minutes, then strain as above. Makes about 1 cup liquid.

SNACKS

In Caracas, be sure to taste the fresh fruit sherbets made from local fruits: guava, mango and tamarindo are just a few. A snack you can duplicate at home is Tostados (on p. 109). For Tostadas, start with an Arepa made from cornmeal, then stuff with any of the fillings you'll find listed for empanadas in the Buenos Aires section. In Venezuela, women grind their own corn for arepas or go completely modern and use a package mix.

Spanish and Indian cultures, the lifeblood of Lima, are now mixed with 20th-century vitality that is determined to make Lima one of the most important cities on the continent. Limeñans are fiercely proud of their heritage. The Plaza de Armas with its old cathedral, and Torre Tagle Palace are places to see Spanish colonial influence. To understand Inca greatness, start with the Museum of Art and Archaeology; follow with a trip to Cuzco, ancient Inca capital, and Machu Picchu.

PICNICS

Cuzco and Machu Picchu, the ancient Inca ruins, would hardly be likely picnic excursions, yet a pleasant way to picnic is to visit other ruins just 45 minutes southwest of Lima. Travel another mile or so to marvel at the Indian road, built a thousand years ago, linking Lima with Cuzco. Your picnic could include two different potato salads — nothing like our American ones.

PERUVIAN CAUSA

Serves 8

3 pounds sweet potatoes, cooked and peeled
1 tablespoon lemon juice
1 teaspoon salt
1/8 teaspoon hot pepper sauce
2 cloves garlic, pressed
1/2 cup finely chopped onion
1/4 cup chopped pimiento-stuffed olives
1/4 cup chopped parsley
3 tablespoons oil
3 tablespoons vinegar

Above: Snacktime on the streets of Lima is a busy time; outdoor stalls make food handy.

Mash potatoes with lemon juice, salt and hot pepper sauce. Form into 16 balls about the size of small lemons. Place in Cold Cut Keeper. Combine remaining ingredients and sprinkle over potato balls. Serve garnished with pieces of avocado, shrimp, hard-cooked egg, lettuce and cooked corn. Refrigerate until ready to serve.

POTATO HUANCAINA

Serves 6

2 pounds potatoes, cooked, peeled, cut in small pieces
½ cup chopped scallion
½ cup smooth peanut butter
½ cup boiling water
¼ cup sour cream
¼ cup vinegar
2 cloves garlic
1 teaspoon salt
¼ teaspoon pepper
dash tabasco
¼ cup sliced red pimientos

Combine potatoes and scallions in a 3-quart Wonderlier. Combine remaining ingredients, except pimiento, in a 2-cup Wonderlier. Let stand at least 2 hours. Combine potatoes and dressing. Stir in pimiento. Serve on lettuce garnished with tomato slices.

PARTIES

Lima offers more variety in food than any other South American city. Our party recipes are an excellent sampling of the many kinds of foods to be tasted. The Indians have given Peru an abundance of corn — some 155 varieties — and there are many imaginative party uses: Peruvians eat small cobs of corn cold as an appetizer, they grill it on wooden skewers, they use purple corn in a tasty dessert.

DUCK CUZCO

Serves 4 to 6

5 to 6 pound duckling, cut in small pieces
4 tablespoons oil
½ cup chopped onion
1 clove garlic, minced
1 tablespoon ground coriander
1 teaspoon ground cumin
1 12-ounce bottle dark beer
1½ cups white rice
1 large tomato cut in 6 wedges
1 hot pepper cut in 6 slices

Sauté duckling in oil until brown on all sides. Remove from skillet and pour off all but 2 tablespoons of fat. Add onion and garlic, cook until soft but not brown. Add spices, duckling and 1 quart water. Simmer, covered, 1½ hours or until duckling is tender. Set aside. Pour beer into large saucepan. Add ½ of the duck liquid and enough water to make 2½ cups of liquid. Bring to a boil, add rice and 1 teaspoon salt. Turn heat low and cover rice. Simmer 12 to 15 minutes or until rice is tender and liquid absorbed. Heat duckling in remaining sauce. Serve duckling and additional sauce over rice. Garnish each serving with a section of tomato and a piece of hot pepper.

Take Peruvian potato salads on a picnic.

LAMB LAS TRECE MONEDAS

Serves 8 to 10

4 tablespoons flour

1 teaspoon salt

½ teaspoon black pepper

5 to 6 pound boneless leg of lamb, cut in 1½-inch cubes

4 tablespoons butter

¼ cup chopped onion

1 clove garlic, finely chopped

2 teaspoons ground cumin

2 teaspoons ground coriander

¼ teaspoon crushed dried red peppers

1 cup white wine

1 cup bouillon

Combine flour, salt and black pepper, use to coat lamb cubes. Melt butter in large saucepan. Add lamb and brown on all sides. Add onion and garlic and sauté until tender, but not brown. Add remaining ingredients and simmer, covered, 45 minutes or until meat is tender.

Check during cooking and add more broth if necessary. Serve with white rice, corn, beans, potatoes and hot pepper.

SUSPIRO LEMINO

Serves 6

2¼ cups white sugar
6 egg yolks
1 13-ounce can (about 1 cup) evaporated milk, heated
2 teaspoons vanilla extract
⅛ teaspoon cream of tartar
¼ cup water
¼ cup sweet white wine
2 egg whites (about ¼ cup)

Beat 1½ cups sugar with egg yolks until light and creamy. Add the heated milk gradually to the egg yolks, beating constantly. Return mixture to saucepan; cook over very low heat, stirring constantly until the custard coats the spoon. Remove from heat and stir in 1 teaspoon vanilla. Pour into a 3-quart Wonderlier. Combine the sugar, cream of tartar, water and wine in saucepan. Stir and cook over low heat until it boils. Cover and boil 3 minutes, or until steam washes down any crystals on side of pan. Boil without stirring until syrup reaches 242°F. or jelly stage. Beat egg whites until stiff, gradually beat in syrup until mixture stands in stiff peaks. Beat in vanilla. Spread meringue over custard, chill thoroughly, serve very cold.

This is a smooth, creamy, slightly soft crème brûlée type custard, with the most tender, tasty meringue ever invented. The custard is really a thick sauce.

SNACKS

Throughout Lima, you will see little snack wagons where a "cassera" dispenses food. Nibble on sandwiches garnished with fried sweet potatoes or try Aceituna Cebolla Queso Fresco, a combination of black olives, onions and fresh cheese, cottage variety. At dusk, charcoal fires light up Lima; Anticuchos, grilled beef hearts or shrimp, are the tidbits to be sampled at charcoal stands and duly noted for at-home snacking.

ANTICUCHOS MIXED PERUVIAN GRILL

Serves 6

2 cups olive oil
1 cup lemon juice
1 clove garlic, minced
1 bay leaf
½ teaspoon salt
½ teaspoon monosodium glutamate
2 pounds veal heart
2 pounds boneless steak, cut in ½-inch cubes
¼ cup butter
1 onion, minced
1 clove garlic, minced
½ cup flour
2½ cups chicken stock, heated
1 bouillon cube
1 tablespoon chili powder

Combine first 6 ingredients in Cold Cut Keeper. Wash heart, cut out arteries and veins at the top and inside the heart. Cut into ¼-inch cubes. Place on 24 bamboo skewers alternately with beef cubes. Place in marinade in Cold Cut Keeper; marinate at least 2 hours. For sauce, melt butter in saucepan. Add onion and garlic, cook until tender. Add flour, stirring constantly until well blended. Gradually add stock, a little at a time, stirring constantly. Add chili and simmer sauce 20 minutes, making a medium-thick sauce. Strain and season to taste (hot pepper sauce may be added if a hotter sauce is desired). Store sauce in 2-cup Wonderlier until ready to serve with meat. Anticuchos may also be made just with shrimp, as our photograph shows. Simply marinate in sauce and grill until done.

Typical Peruvian desserts: top, left is our Suspiro Lemiño.

Montevideo

Uruguay, the smallest of the South American republics, is too little-known and visited. It is a friendly country and its capital city, Montevideo, is a place of gracious homes, modern apartment houses and good restaurants. In season, Montevideo offers the finest resort living, with a string of beautiful beaches and lively outdoor sidewalk cafés. At any time of the year, you'll want to take an excursion to an estancia to watch the gauchos—South American cowboys—at work.

PICNICS

Punta del Este, Uruguay's most famous seaside resort, a three-hour drive from Montevideo, is a perfect target for a day's excursion. Swim, relax, then picnic on Fiambre, a flank-steak loaf filled with eggs and peas. For those summer weekends when guests are expected and the schedule is hectic, keep Fiambre in the refrigerator, invite guests to help themselves to lunch.

FIAMBRE (ROLLED FLANK STEAK)

Serves 6

5 eggs
⅓ cup grated Cheddar cheese
2 tablespoons butter
1 3-pound flank steak
½ teaspoon salt
½ teaspoon pepper
1 small pimiento, diced
½ cup cooked green peas
6 cups beef broth

Beat eggs and cheese together. Melt butter in skillet, add egg mixture and cook, stirring constantly, until eggs are dry. Sprinkle salt and pepper on flank steak. Cover with cooked eggs, pimiento and peas. Roll from short side and sew with string. Wrap in cheesecloth and sew again. Place in large saucepan and add stock. Bring to a boil, skim and turn heat down. Simmer, covered, 1½ to 2 hours, or until steak is tender. Remove from stock and press with a heavy object. Cool in Bread Server. Cut in slices and serve with vegetables marinated in a vinaigrette sauce.

A very attractive, tasty dish. The filling retains its shape very well and each slice is a perfect circle of meat with a center of egg and peas.

PARTIES

A stew that is good enough for a party; a new touch for standard roast beef; an impressive cake with only the meringue to bake — these are the three unhackneyed party suggestions imported from Montevideo. The meat and stew are hearty winter fare; the cake is light and delicious enough to be served any time. It has such a handsome and festive air, it could easily be the star of a shower, an anniversary or a birthday party.

ASADO CON GUERO

Serves 8 to 10

½ cup oil
2 onions finely chopped (about 1 cup)
2 tablespoons chili powder
1 tablespoon salt
3 cloves garlic, minced
1 5-pound rolled rib roast
Chimichurria Sauce (recipe below)

Combine first five ingredients and spread on roast. Place in Fix-N-Mix and marinate 4 to 6 hours. Roast in 325°F. oven 2 to 2½ hours, or until meat thermometer reads 140° for rare or 150° for medium rare. Serve with sauce.

CHIMICHURRIA SAUCE

3 cloves garlic, minced
3 gherkins, chopped
3 pimientos, finely chopped
2 carrots, peeled and diced
1 onion finely chopped
½ cup finely chopped parsley
½ cup water
¼ cup vinegar
3 tablespoons oil
1 tablespoon capers
1 teaspoon salt
1 teaspoon ground pepper
½ teaspoon ground chili

Combine all ingredients in saucepan. Simmer, covered, 30 minutes. Add more water during cooking period if necessary.

A different touch for the standard roast beef – the tangy, vinegarish sauce really makes it an interesting dish. Sauce is like a built-in relish for the meat.

CARBONADA CRIOLLA

Serves 8 to 10

¼ cup flour
1 teaspoon salt
1 teaspoon pepper

3 pounds boneless shoulder of veal, cut in 1½ inch cubes
¼ cup butter
2 cups beef bouillon
1 cup white wine
1½ pounds potatoes, peeled and quartered (about 4 cups cubes)
2 pears, peeled, cut in large pieces
2 peaches, peeled, quartered
2 ears corn, cut in 1-inch pieces
½ pound pumpkin, cut in 2-inch cubes (about 1 cup cubes)
½ pound carrots, peeled, quartered
1 apple, peeled, cut in large pieces
1 onion, chopped (about ½ cup)
3 tomatoes, quartered
½ cup white rice, cooked

Combine flour, salt and pepper; use to coat veal cubes. Melt butter in large saucepan. Add veal and brown well on all sides. Add liquids and simmer covered 1 hour or until veal is almost done. Add everything but tomatoes and rice. Simmer another 30 minutes. Add tomatoes and cook 15 minutes more or until meat and vegetables are tender. Serve topped with cooked rice.

A mild-flavored stew, different because of the many fruits used. A very good party dish—it goes a long way and is unusual and attractive.

CHAJA

1 10-inch sponge cake
¼ cup peach brandy
1-pound can sliced peaches, drained, finely minced
3 tablespoons chopped candied peel, finely minced
Vanilla Cream (recipe below)
2 cups heavy cream, sweetened and whipped
Meringue Crumbs (recipe below)

Split cake into 3 layers. Sprinkle 1 layer with brandy, cover with ½ the vanilla cream, half the peaches and candied peel. Top with a second layer of cake, vanilla cream, peaches and peel. Top with third layer of cake. Frost top and sides with sweet-

Shrimp Brochette with pungent Aioli Sauce.

ened whipped cream. Sprinkle entire cake with meringue crumbs.

VANILLA CREAM

5 cups

10 egg yolks
2 cups granulated sugar
1⅓ cups sifted flour
1 quart boiling milk
3 tablespoons vanilla extract
2 tablespoons butter

Beat egg yolks until thick and lemon colored. Gradually add sugar, beating constantly, until mixture is pale yellow. Beat in

flour. Gradually add boiling milk, a little at a time, beating constantly. Pour into saucepan, cook over moderate heat, stirring constantly, until thick. Remove from heat, beat in vanilla, butter.

MERINGUE

6 egg whites (about 1 cup)
½ teaspoon cream of tartar
2 cups sugar

Combine egg whites and cream of tartar, beat until frothy. Add sugar, a little at a time, beating constantly until whites are stiff and glossy. Cover a cookie sheet with brown paper. Spread with meringue. Bake in 250°F. oven 1¼ hours. Cool and crumble.

SNACKS

Chivito—a small steak sandwich on hamburger roll, garnished with lettuce, mayonnaise and chopped onion — is a favorite snack. Two other ideas from Montevideo that can be adopted for snacking are Shrimp Brochette and Spaghetti Roquefort. Both take little time to prepare and cook. The spaghetti is perfect to serve drop-in company for dinner. The Shrimp with Aioli Sauce makes a good end to a lazy summer afternoon.

SHRIMP BROCHETTE VICTORIA PLAZA

Serves 4

1 pound cleaned, deveined shrimp
½ teaspoon salt
⅛ teaspoon paprika
4 slices trimmed toast, buttered
Aioli Sauce (recipe below)

Season shrimp with salt and paprika, place on skewers. Broil 10 minutes, or until thoroughly cooked. Serve on a whole loaf of toasted bread, or on individual slices of toast, with Aioli Sauce.

AIOLI SAUCE

5 cloves, finely minced
1 egg yolk
¼ teaspoon salt
1 cup plus 3 tablespoons oil
2 tablespoons lemon juice
1 tablespoon warm water

Have all ingredients except water very cold. Mash garlic to a pulp in a small mortar. Add egg yolk and salt. Beat until thick and lemon colored. Add the 3 tablespoons oil very, very slowly, drop by drop, beating constantly. Gradually add the lemon juice and water, beating constantly. Mix in remaining oil while beating constantly, drop by drop at first and then in a gradually increasing amount as the mixture thickens. Store in a 2-cup Wonderlier. Serve chilled.

SPAGHETTI ROQUEFORT

Serves 4

¼ cup butter (½ stick)
4 ounces Roquefort cheese
1 cup tomato sauce

Melt butter over low heat, add cheese and stir until well blended. Add tomato sauce and cook until mixture is thoroughly heated. Serve over spaghetti.

Bogotá

From the peak of Monserrate, reached by cable car, there's a glorious view of modern Bogota, a city some 8,000 feet above sea level. You can still see narrow, winding streets with traces of Spanish influence in the old part of town, but it is Bogota's bustling air of being part of the 20th century that is most impressive. Cartagena, a city dating back to 1533, is the Colombian city where the old world in many guises can still be enjoyed. This Caribbean city is also famous for its fine beaches.

PARTIES

If you serve family meat favorites in the same old way week after week, everyone is sure to tire of them. Nothing is more boring than weekday meal sameness. Try our recipes for loin of pork and brisket of beef with company manners. It's the typical Colombian use of seasonings that enhances the flavor of the pork and the beef. Both dishes are easy to prepare.

Above: Chicken Soup Tequendama Style: rich with sweet potatoes, cream, special seasoning.

SOBREBARRIGA

Serves 8 to 10

1 4-pound brisket of beef
1½ cups beer (1 12-ounce can)
1 bay leaf
1 clove garlic, minced
½ teaspoon thyme
¼ teaspoon ground cumin
⅛ teaspoon pepper
2 tablespoons butter
2 tablespoons flour

Place beef in Square Keeper, add

beer, bay leaf, garlic, thyme, cumin and pepper. Cover and marinate in refrigerator overnight. Next day remove meat from marinade, dry well. Melt butter in large saucepan, add meat and brown well on all sides; add marinade and simmer, covered, 2 to 2½ hours or until tender. Remove meat and strain gravy. Skim fat, thicken gravy with the 2 tablespoons flour. Slice meat and return to gravy, heat thoroughly.

A very tasty, hearty pot roast, excellent brown gravy. This freezes very well. Serve half, freeze rest in Snack Stor.

LOMO DE CERDO

Serves 6 to 10

1 4 to 5 pound loin of pork
2 cups beef broth
1 cup water
2 bunches scallions, minced (about 2 cups)
1 clove garlic, minced
1 teaspoon salt
½ teaspoon ground cumin
3 tablespoons butter
1 tablespoon flour
¼ teaspoon saffron

Place pork in large saucepan. Add broth, water, 1 cup scallions, garlic, salt and cumin. Bring to boil and simmer, covered, 1½ hours, or until tender. Remove pork and cut into 1-inch cubes. Strain cooking liquid, skim fat and reserve 1 cup of broth. Melt butter in skillet, add remaining scallions and sauté 2 minutes. Add flour and stir until well blended. Gradually add reserved broth, stirring constantly. Add saffron and cook over low heat until sauce thickens slightly. Blend with pork cubes and place in 350°F. oven until meat is hot and sauce bubbles, about 10 minutes. Serve with rice. Pork may be garnished with pimientos if desired.

SNACKS

In Colombia, coffee, of course, is the between-meals refreshment. In fact, as many as 10 demitasses may be consumed between breakfast and lunch. With coffee, Bunelos, a type of donut, or Pan de Yuca, a cheese roll, is eaten. Our two Colombian soups make good snack meals. Accompany the Crab Soup with toasted cheese bread and watercress-endive-beet salad. The Chicken Soup — a meal in a bowl — goes nicely with avocado vinaigrette.

CHICKEN SOUP TEQUENDAMA STYLE

Serves 6 to 8

1 3-pound chicken, cut in serving pieces
6 small onions
1½ teaspoons salt
1 teaspoon ground coriander
1 teaspoon ground cumin
5 medium potatoes, peeled, quartered
3 medium sweet potatoes, peeled, quartered
6 corn on cob, cut in 2-inch pieces
1 cup light cream

Place chicken in large kettle, cover with 2½ quarts water. Bring to a boil and skim. Add onions and spices, cover and simmer 20 minutes. Add vegetables and simmer, covered, 20 minutes more. Add cream and serve.

CRAB SOUP

Serves 4 to 6

1 dozen hard shell crabs (about 2½ pounds)
2 cups chicken broth
2 cups water
1 tablespoon butter
1 tablespoon cream
⅛ teaspoon gravy seasoning

Scrub crabs to remove all dirt. Place in large saucepan with broth and water. Simmer 15 minutes, cool and store overnight, refrigerated, in a 3-quart Wonderlier. Next day crack shells and pick meat from crabs, reserving 4 claws for garnish. Measure broth and add enough water to make 3 cups liquid. Place in saucepan with crab meat, claws, butter, cream and gravy seasoning; simmer 10 minutes. Correct seasoning. Serve hot.

A hearty broth with a true crab flavor.

Crab Soup—inspected by chief ingredient.

Rio de Janeiro

Everyone with a yearning to travel dreams of visiting Rio, the carnival city. Somehow Rio manages to be informal, convivial, bent on having fun without sacrificing its sophisticated, cosmopolitan ambience. Take a cable car up to Sugar Loaf to gape at the view, visit nearby Ipanema to watch the surfers, soak up sun on Copacabana Beach—it is perfectly acceptable to get there, as the Brazilians do, as early as 6 a.m. Shopping for semi-precious stones — another irresistible attraction.

PICNICS

The Brazilians don't picnic as we do. They are fond of barbecuing, however, with such recipes as Brazilian Mixed Grill. Mary Martin, the famous stage star, has a coffee plantation near Brasilia. She and her husband, Richard Halliday, do picnic there, usually on horseback, carrying lunch in saddlebags. They take fruits that they grow: pau-pau melon and pineapples.

BRAZILIAN MIXED GRILL ON A SKEWER

Serves 6

1 pound boneless steak, cut into 12 cubes, sautéed

1 pound boneless pork, cut into 12 cubes, cooked 10 minutes

1 pound boneless lamb, cut into 12 cubes

6 spicy sausage (Spanish sausage if possible) cut in half

2 ears corn, cut into 3 sections each

Farofa (recipe below)

Picnic on Copacabana Beach—in the background, colorful bird kites.

Place ingredients on a skewer in the following order: sausage, beef, lamb, pork, corn. Repeat, placing two pieces of each kind of meat on skewer. Serve with Farofa.

FAROFA

½ pound (about 12 slices) bacon, minced
3 cups (12 ounces) manioc flour
6 eggs
2 tablespoons milk
10 ounces Cheddar cheese, diced
10 scallions, diced
1 red onion, diced
salt
pepper
3 tablespoons butter

Cook bacon in large frypan until crisp; add manioc flour and brown lightly, stirring constantly. Beat eggs with milk. Add remaining ingredients except butter. Melt 3 tablespoons butter in large frypan. Add egg mixture and manioc, cook over moderate heat until eggs are set. Serve with hot mixed grill.

The Farofa really makes this dish. The skewers are fun because they are not the same old shish kabob, but the Farofa is a crunchy, tasty and attractive side dish.

PARTIES

Parties in Rio are known to go on and on. The hostess who invites guests for hors d'oeuvres may also wind up serving them breakfast. Picadinho is an excellent, filling party dish to have on hand for just such an emergency. The ingredients can be kept ready in refrigerator in Square Rounds. Actual cooking time is just a few minutes.

PICADINHO

Serves 2 to 3

2 tablespoons butter
1 pound filet mignon or boneless sirloin, cut into ½-inch cubes
2 tomatoes, diced
2 pitted black olives, chopped
2 hard-cooked eggs, chopped

Heat butter in frypan. Add meat and cook until brown, about 2 minutes. Remove and set aside. Add onion and tomatoes and simmer 2 minutes. Add meat, cook until done to degree desired. Season to taste. Serve sprinkled with olives and eggs.

Very tasty, nice change of pace for a steak meal.

FEIJOADA

Serves 8 to 10

4 pounds pork roast
5 cloves garlic
2 bay leaves
1 pound dried kidney beans
2 pigs knuckles
2 carrots
1 stalk celery
1 leek
5 cloves
5 peppercorns
3 onions
2 teaspoons salt

Brown pork in large skillet on top of stove. Chop 1 clove garlic and sprinkle over pork. Roast in 325°F. oven 2 hours, or until meat thermometer reads 180°F. Wash beans well, place in 2-

quart Wonderlier, soak 3 or 4 hours. Drain beans. Place in large kettle with 8 cups water; bring to boil and skim foam. Add pigs knuckles. Put bay leaves, carrots, celery, leek, cloves, garlic and peppercorns in cheesecloth, tie tightly and place in beans. Add onions. Cover and let simmer 3 to 4 hours or until beans are tender and water absorbed. Discard vegetable-spice bouquet. Trim meat from knuckles and return meat to beans. Dice cooked pork and stir into beans. Heat, serve with rice.

Feijoada can be considered the national dish of Brazil, usually served as a Saturday luncheon because it is heavy.

SNACKS

Rio and its Copacabana Beach, with the famous mosaic sidewalks, is one of the greatest walking places in the world. It's great sport to sit at an open-air sidewalk café and watch the world go by. Here's where you can drink tiny cups of rich, dark coffee with a delicious cake, Papos de Anjo. The Brazilians drink coffee continuously, at least every hour on the hour. Toast and chocolate milk is another locally favored snack.

PAPOS DE ANJO

Makes 18

12 egg yolks
1 egg white
2 cups sugar
3½ cups water
1 teaspoon vanilla extract

Beat yolks and egg white 20 minutes at moderate speed with an electric mixer, until yolks are very thick and lemon colored. Pour 2 tablespoons of mixture into lightly greased ¼-cup baking tins (or use small custard cups). Place in a pan of hot water; bake in 325°F. oven 30 minutes. Combine sugar and water in medium saucepan. Bring to a boil and simmer 5 minutes. Add vanilla, remove from heat. When Papos are baked, gently remove from tins. Drop into warm syrup and turn to coat thoroughly. Gently remove each cake from syrup and place on a plate or in Cold Cut Keeper to cool. When both Papos and syrup are thoroughly cold, serve Papos in Sauce Dish covered with syrup. Serve 3 per person.

These are light, airy, spongy and delightful, rather like eating sweet air. Very unusual and attractive.

AVOCADO BRASILIA A LA MARY MARTIN

2 avocados (about 2 cups, mashed)
3 tablespoons fresh lime or lemon juice
sugar to taste (optional)
1 cup vanilla ice cream
fresh mint
grated lemon, lime or orange peel

Mash avocados and put through a strainer. Add juice of lime or lemon to taste (with or without sugar). Mix strained avocados with ice cream and keep in freezer until ready to serve. Sprinkle finely chopped fresh mint, with grated lemon, lime or orange peel, on top of each serving.

BUENOS AIRES

Buenos Aires is the most European of all the South American cities; it's not unlike Paris in tempo, with handsome streets like Plaza San Martin, and tempting high-style shopping areas like Calle Florida. La Boca, a wharfside district, has quite another flavor. Here the houses and everything inside—from light switches to banisters—are painted bright primary colors. If time allows, visit Bariloche for skiing, Mar del Plata, the *beach resort, and Iguassu Falls, higher than our Niagara.*

PARTIES

Parrillada, the combination of beef, sausage and kidneys, ranks high on the list of Argentine party dishes. However, do try other specialties. Bife a Caballo, or steak on horseback, is steak with two fried eggs. Puchero, a hearty stew, is similar to our New England boiled dinner and utilizes typically South American vegetables in an interesting, savory way.

Above, Puchero: the Argentinian version of New England boiled dinner.

PUCHERO

Serves 8 to 10

2 pounds chuck, cut in 1½-inch cubes
1 chicken (3½ pounds) disjointed
½ pound bacon, diced
½ pound spicy sausages (chorizo if possible)
1 pound carrots, cleaned, cut in 2-inch lengths
4 stalks celery, cut in 2-inch lengths
2 pounds white potatoes, cut in quarters
1 pound sweet potatoes, peeled, quartered
4 corn on the cob, cut in 2-inch pieces

1 cabbage, cut in eighths
4 ripe plantains, cut in 2-inch sections
1 pound yellow squash, cut in 2-inch circles
2 cups (1-pound 4-ounce can) drained chick peas

Place meats except sausage in large kettle, cover with 4 quarts water. Bring to a boil; skim, simmer 1½ hours. Add carrots, celery, sausage, and potatoes; simmer 30 minutes more. Add remaining ingredients and simmer 20 minutes, or until cabbage is tender. Taste for seasoning. Remove meats and vegetables and arrange on large serving platter. Serve the soup in separate bowls.

PICNICS, SNACKS

September 21st, the first day of spring, is a holiday. People picnic in Palermo Park or drive out of town to Tigre. The park is crowded with teenagers who play soccer, ride in boats, crowd into horsedrawn carriages. Sausage and baby beef on hard rolls are two favorite sandwiches. Empanadas are the favorite snack, with many restaurants selling empanadas exclusively. In Argentina, each state changes the empanada dough and spicing slightly.

EMPANADA DOUGH

20 large

4 ounces lard, softened
2¾ cups flour
2 tablespoons oil
3 eggs
½ cup water

Whip lard until light and fluffy. Add flour, mix thoroughly. Add oil, two eggs and mix well. Add water, a little at a time, stirring constantly, until dough is smooth. Flour hands and place dough on floured Pastry Sheet. Knead lightly until dough no longer sticks to hands. Place in 4-cup Wonderlier, cover and refrigerate 1 hour. Remove from refrigerator and roll out on well-floured board. Roll to 1/16-inch thickness. Cut out rounds of 6-inch diameter. Fill with any of the filling recipes that follow, using about 2 tablespoons mixture per round. Beat remaining egg and brush edge of each circle. Fold dough in half to form half-moon shape. Pinch edges tightly and twist ends slightly away from closed side to form half moon. Fry in deep, hot oil (375° F.) until golden. Drain on absorbent paper and serve hot.

SEAFOOD FILLING

2 cups

¼ cup butter
¼ cup chopped shallots
3 ounces shrimp, shelled, cleaned, cut in 1-inch pieces
3 ounces crab meat
3 ounces lobster, cut in 1-inch pieces
¼ cup sherry
2 tablespoons butter
¾ cup flour
1 cup plus 2 tablespoons light cream, heated
½ teaspoon salt

Melt ¼ cup butter in large frypan. Sauté shallots until light brown; add seafood and stir well. Add sherry, blend and set mixture aside. Melt 2 table-

La Boca—Buenos Aires' colorful wharfside district.

spoons butter, add flour and stir well. Let simmer over very low heat 2 or 3 minutes to cook flour. Gradually add warm cream, beating constantly. Bring to boil and strain sauce. Pour over prepared fish and mix well.

BEEF FILLING

2½ cups

- 6 teaspoons cooking oil
- ¼ cup minced onion
- ½ green pepper, seeded, cut in strips
- ¾ pound ground beef
- 1 small clove garlic, mashed
- ½ teaspoon salt
- 1 tomato, chopped
- 2 tablespoons raisins
- 2 tablespoons chopped olives

Heat oil in large frypan. Sauté onions and green pepper until tender. Add meat, garlic and salt, cook until brown. Remove from heat and stir in remaining ingredients.

PORK FILLING

2 cups

- 1 small tomato, peeled and chopped
- ¼ cup minced onion
- 2 tablespoons raisins
- 1 clove garlic, minced
- 2 tablespoons cooking oil
- ½ pound cooked, diced pork
- ¼ cup sliced pimiento-stuffed olives
- 2 hard-cooked eggs, chopped
- ¼ teaspoon salt

Combine tomato, onion, raisins and garlic, sauté in oil for 5 minutes. Combine with remaining ingredients.

PICNICKING 'ROUND THE WORLD

Everyone will recognize the classic image of the European traveler, stopping along the road near some small French village to picnic sumptuously on a loaf of bread, a country pâté and a bottle of wine of the region.

Many of us who travel extensively never get to that little village but there's no need to forego the joys of picnicking. There are many reasons to picnic while traveling—and here we use the term picnic to mean anything less than a formal meal in a restaurant. Herewith a sort of diary of the "why" of our Picnic Kit and how we used it:

You can picnic—and well—going totally unprepared. We, however, set out armed—but lightly—with a Pan Am flight bag filled with our picnic equipment.

The Kit held Tupperware containers: a Bread Server, a large shape that held everything from cold lobsters in Puerto Rico to calzoni in Rome; a Handolier to carry juices or drinks; two Tumblers; two Cereal Bowls; two Square Rounds and a Salt and Pepper Shaker. The Cereal Bowls and Square Rounds are dual purpose—both carriers and individual plates.

Another must is a good can opener—mine is also a corkscrew, one I found in Spain. Other picnic equipment includes the following Boy Scout items: two sets of utensils—knife, fork and spoon that come in their own plastic holder; a metal match holder; a 4-x-3-inch portable stove that comes with its own dry fuel and can heat a small serving of a can of anything in just a few minutes. Get a metal one-cup-size saucepan for this. The portable stove fits in the palm of your hand and weighs next to nothing. We used it many times. In Bangkok, it heated a can of frogs' legs I carried along with other French goodies all the way from Paris. This made a nice change-of-pace food in the Orient.

Invariably, the picnic menu offered at hotels will be ham and cheese sandwiches, hard-boiled eggs and fruit. Nothing wrong with that—but why not take individual salads, a pastry dessert and a refreshing fruit drink? The range of food you order from the hotel for a picnic and the food you can buy immediately become more varied with our Picnic Kit.

When not holding food, the Tupperware containers were used to separate all the travel accessories that usually are lumped together in one mess. Pills and medicines; hand care and manicure items; stamps and stationery were stored in their own containers.

In the shadow of the Parthenon,
the Tupperware Picnic Kit.

WHEN TO PICNIC

THE ALL-DAY OUTING

If you're off on an all-day trip, you may not want to take the time in the middle of the day to stop at a restaurant. Or there may be only one "tourist acceptable" restaurant, invariably jammed at the noon hour.

In Geneva, we had a late breakfast and would not reach our destination in the mountains until 3 p.m., too late for the local restaurants to serve lunch. We picnicked on "Viande Sechée des Grisons"—the Swiss specialty. This is meat of mountain cattle which is steeped in red wine and dried in the open air high in the Alps. Sliced paper thin, it is eaten with bread and butter, pickles and small white onions.

On our way from Beirut to Ba'albek, we didn't want to miss the daylight hours for photography, so our lunch was at 4 p.m. When we stopped for a cool drink in Ferzol, the proprietor of the roadside restaurant insisted we bring our lunch and sit at an outdoor table. There then followed a convivial exchange of hospitality. He gave me a piece of gum, I reciprocated with a hard-boiled egg, he gave me some chocolate wafers, and so on.

The Lebanese, just as we do, love to go to the country on Sunday. You can see droves of them sitting on camp stools picnicking. They also stop at orchards for oranges and bananas and at country bakeries for the delicious, freshly baked flat bread.

THOSE BIG LUNCHES

Few of us can resist eating big lunches when we're traveling. Then, if we're smart, we relax an hour or so before an evening out—perhaps a performance of the Royal Ballet in Copenhagen is on tap. Something to eat is in order, but nothing heavy. One possibility in Copenhagen is a "canned picnic." One we tried in our Copenhagen hotel is put up in a cylindrical box called, of all things, "The Tourist." Every country has some specialties available in cans that are perfect for relaxed snacking.

HOLIDAY AWAY FROM HOME

Nostalgia seizes any tourist away from home on an important holiday but you'll undoubtedly find our holiday food duplicated everywhere. We were in Athens on Thanksgiving and enjoyed a fine turkey dinner with all the trimmings at our hotel.

Perhaps eating in a restaurant is the last thing on your mind on a holiday. We had a most acceptable Christmas dinner-holiday picnic we assembled at Fortnum & Mason: a smoked turkey, plum pudding, fruit and nuts—the works.

WHEN THE CHILDREN ARE WITH YOU

I first realized how practical picnicking could be when we took our boys to Europe—at the time, they were 4, 10, and 11. They are excellent travelers, but they couldn't cope with the 9 p.m. or later dinner hour of Lisbon. Solution: our English-speaking driver directed us to places where we could buy supper. I remember a delicious roasted chicken purchased in a large, impressive food shop right across the street from the main beach at Estoril. After a hearty lunch and a day's swimming or sightseeing, the boys were happy to settle for a "picnic" in our room and an early bedtime. Next trip, I'll stash away some dry cereal for when they start to balk at croissants for breakfast.

THE CHANGE-OF-PACE PICNIC

If you're on a budget, the change-of-pace picnic is meant to be a splurge. It can be a small-in-price indiscretion like the luscious Fruit Tart from Fauchon's in Paris, but it should be elegant eating. You can buy such food in luxury food shops all over the world.

If you're not on a budget, your change-of-pace picnic should be food not found in the posh restaurants. A trip to a German bakery and sausage shop might be just the thing.

WHERE TO BUY YOUR PICNIC 'ROUND THE WORLD

AMSTERDAM

Even if you decide to go picnicking at the last minute, Mouwes is a store that is open on Sundays. Try Farmer's worst, Aalbessen (berries), delicious raisin buns, Rookvlees (smoked, paper-thin beef), sliced boiled liver and, of course, some raw herring. The old standbys will also be offered to you, like ham and liverwurst — but why not go Dutch?

ATHENS

Zonars (near Constitution Square), Psitas (near University Avenue), and Vassilatos (near Stadium Avenue) are combination bakery-delicatessen-grocery stores. Buy spinach pie, cheese pie, Greek peasant salad, Kalamata olives, Feta or Kasseri cheese.

COPENHAGEN

In Copenhagen, go to a Viktualieforretning for lobster salad, liver pâté, Esrom and Havarti cheese, Rullepølse (a rectangular sausage), herring, hard-boiled eggs, salami. Strawberries, which the Danes love and eat in abundance, are in season from mid-June to mid-July. You can also take out prepared Danish open sandwiches.

FRANKFURT

When you head for the mountains of Germany on a picnic, your knapsack will be stuffed with Wiener Schnitzel (breaded veal to be eaten cold), and hearty German sausages such as knackwurst and teewurst. Potato salad and sweet-sour pickles are other favorites.

GENEVA

In Switzerland, it's fun to picnic at one of the Fests held throughout the year. There are music fests, open air dancing fests, even yodel fests. A chef usually presides over the roasting of sausage. On a Swiss picnic, you are also likely to enjoy a sausage salad and air-dried meats (Bindenfleisch), along with a variety of cheese available in individual portions. A chain of butcher shops, named Bell, is a good place to buy a variety of cold cuts and sausages. Be sure you also take along individual squares of Swiss chocolate.

LONDON

The British way to go on a picnic is to fill your hamper with sandwiches of watercress, marmite (a vegetable spread), cucumber, etc. Drink lemon squash or tea. Add a sweet for dessert, such as fruitcake or a sponge cake, and you have a jolly good meal. In London, you might enjoy the British version of an American tailgate picnic. At the Glyndebourne Opera, everyone picnics during the intermission. The menu might include: Melton Mowbray Pie (ham pie), Veal and Ham Pie, cold roasted chicken or turkey, butter and rolls, champagne, and trifle for dessert. Fortnum & Mason and Harrods are two outstanding stores that sell gourmet picnic food.

PARIS

At a charcuterie you'll find many kinds of pâté, salamis, salads that are home made. French canned food, to be eaten hot or cold, is superb. So is the bread—many French people go to a bakery twice a day to have really fresh bread. Cheeses are not found in charcuteries but in dairy shops (crémerie), or groceries or supermarkets. Some of the best known and most delicious of the French cheeses to try in France: Camembert, Brie, Pont l'Eveque, Gruyere, Cantal, Port Salut, Reblochon.

BEIRUT

The Lebanese are fond of picnicking on Kibbeh—raw lamb, liver or beef – with Tabbouleh salad (parsley and wheat germ). Goat cheese, olives, Arabic bread and the national drink, arak, constitute a typical outdoor meal. Mashed chick peas with sesame oil can also be added to the menu. There are many stores where you can buy rotisserie chickens.

MELBOURNE

Picnic bound, the Australians usually head toward the water, either beach or poolside. Picnics are geared to barbecuing chops and steaks and sausages. However, sandwiches are not outlawed, nor is cold roast chicken. Australians picnic elegantly at country race meetings, horseraces and polo tournaments. Tables, covered with fine linens, are set up in front of Rolls Royces and delicacies like oysters, crab or shrimp are heartily consumed.

SINGAPORE

Outdoors, Singapore's eating stalls are a unique eating experience, not to be missed. Sample everything from satay to a complete curry dinner. Visit Koek Road for Chinese specialties; Beach Road for Malaysian dishes.

ROME

The traveler in Rome can find plenty of places to buy his take-out food for country picnicking or hotel-room snacking. F. Amici, 104 Via Veneto, is one of the many Roman stores equivalent to our better food shops. It carries cold cuts, cheeses and canned goods from every part of the world. If you're homesick for American products, you can find American cereals, canned fruit salad, grapefruit, tomato juice and the like. Euclide, Piazza Euclide 46, is a rosticceria—like our delicatessen, but much finer. The salads displayed in huge trays are particularly appealing—choose from: finocchi and carrot, spinach, cauliflower or beet. Try a mushroom sandwich on green bread, or a fish and egg sandwich on tomato bread. Vitello tonnato, calzoni, spinach and mushroom pies are other possibilities.

HONG KONG

After you have shopped to your heart's content, you will probably long for some peace and quiet away from the crowds. It's not difficult to arrange a relaxing picnic. Yachts are available for rental or you can hike into the countryside. Either your hotel or a local coffee shop has loads of delectables to fill your Picnic Kit. For Jewish food, it's Lindy's East, with pastrami and lox and cream cheese two of the specialties.

MANILA

In the Philippines, picnic on sandwiches of Bandus fish or tongue, adobo of chicken or pork, rice accompanied by mangoes, tomatoes and bananas.

TOKYO

Japanese love to picnic, and in Tokyo the most complicated of picnic or snack menus can be organized in moments. A visit to one of the big food sections of a large Tokyo department store, like Takashimaya, will uncover counter after counter of prepared food—everything from sushi to whole salted fish. You can even pick up one of the famous small, artistically arranged picnic boxes at any of the Tokyo railroad stations. On the trip to Nara or Nikko, nibble on the contents of the picnic box that might contain delicious tamagoyaki (like an omelet), onigiri and sushi.

WILLEMSTAD

Excellent in Curaçao, Zuikertuintje, an old 19th century estate house, sells everything from cold cuts and cheeses to elaborate baked goods. Try Moorkioppen, like a cream puff, or Tompoezen (tom cats), similar to a Napoleon. Visit the floating market—boats from Venezuela tied up at the harbor—for delicious fresh fruit.

SAN JUAN

In San Juan, picnic American style or try food typically Puerto Rican. There are many supermarkets. At Pueblo Food Stores you can choose to go native with pernil sandwiches, tropical salad of cucumbers, avocado, green peppers, radishes or stringbean and chayotes salad. Green plaintains, coconut and pineapple are popular fruits.

CARACAS

Go to a shop that specializes in tostados, a cornmeal-type bread, that can be filled with cold pork roast, Queso Blanco (white cheese) or Queso De Mano. Barbecues are popular in public parks. Yuca — potato substitute — is barbecued along with the steak. Many of the well-to-do Venezuelans own private planes and think nothing of flying a couple of hours into the interior for a Sunday picnic. All the fixings for paella go along, to be cooked over an open fire in a paella pan.

RIO DE JANEIRO

Mercearia is the Brazilian equivalent of our delicatessen, where you'll find European and Brazilian specialties. Try guarana, a local fruit beverage. Visit a local produce market for fruit. There's a big street market that moves to a different part of Rio each day. Prices at 6 a.m. are high, when food is at its freshest, but become progressively lower until the market packs up at noon.

MONTEVIDEO

At a café in Uruguay one can buy food to take out for a picnic: breaded veal, potato salad, Criollo bread, Colonia cheese and sausages for barbecuing. Pick up a tin of Dulce de Membrillo to eat with a slice of cheese, as the Uruguayans do.

BUENOS AIRES

Find one of the many restaurants such as Pulperia La Carcel, Ave. Pte. Quintana 530, that specializes in empanadas. Rotisseries for roasted chicken are, at the present time, also very popular.

BOGOTA

People in Bogota love to picnic. At a Salsamentaria, buy cuajada cheese, guava jelly, roasted chicken or pork and tamales.

Most cities in the United States have neighborhood foreign grocery stores that should be consulted for items not sold at your local supermarket. Any ingredient or equipment not easily available in your city can be mail-ordered from the following stores:

CHEESES: Cheese Unlimited, 1263 Lexington Avenue, New York, New York.
SPANISH & SOUTH AMERICAN: Casa Moneo, 218 West 14 St., New York, New York.
ORIENTAL: Katagiri & Co., Inc., 224 East 59 Street, New York, New York.
MIDDLE EASTERN: Sahadi Import Co., Inc., 187 Atlantic Avenue, Brooklyn, New York.
RACLETTE OVEN: Cheese Unlimited, 1263 Lexington Avenue, New York, New York.
STEAMBOAT or HUO KUO: Cathay Hardware, 49 Mott Street, New York, New York.
MONGOLIAN BARBECUE: The Mandarin House, 133 West 13 St., New York, New York.
HIBACHI: Takashimaya, Inc., 509 Fifth Avenue, New York, New York.

INDEX

A

Page

Anticuchos Mixed Peruvian Grill 116

APPETIZERS
- Baba Ghannouj 56
- Cala 105
- Empanada Dough 130
- Fried Spring Rolls 88
- Hummus Bi Taheeni – Chick Peas with Sesame Oil 54
- Kabiss (Turnip Pickles) 58
- Kesita 103
- Nut and Pâté Sandwiches 45
- Onigiri (Rice Balls) 97
- Pastechi 106
- Roquefort Roulades 76
- Roquefort Sandwiches 45
- Smorrebrod 23
- Tarama 12
- Tostados 109

Asado Con Guero 119

Avgolemono Soup 9

B

Baba Ghannouj 56

Baked Oysters Mornay 61

Banjo Pudding Dessert 100

Bavarian Cream 30

Bavarian Potato Dumplings 28

BEEF
- Anticuchos Mixed Peruvian Grill ... 116
- Asado Con Guero 119
- Beef in Oyster Sauce 71
- Beef Wellington 34
- Bitterballen 15
- Brazilian Mixed Grill 126
- Carpetbag Steak 59
- Fiambre (Rolled Flank Steak) 118
- Kaeng Phed (Meat Curry) 66
- Keshy Yena Curacao Inter Continental 105
- Lasagne Imbottite 48
- Mitzutaki 95
- Mongolian Barbecue 89
- Pabellon 111
- Picadinho 127
- Pie 'n' Sauce – Beef Pie 63
- Puchero 129
- Roast Beef in Crust 34
- Sauerbraten Frankfurt Inter Continental 29
- Sobrebarriga 123
- Steamboat 87
- Stuffed Vine Leaves 13
- Sukiyaki Okura 94
- Tamanaco Carne Asado 110
- Teppan-Yaki 94

Beef in Oyster Sauce 71

Beef Wellington 34

Bienmesabe 112

Bitterballen 15

Bolognese Sauce 49

Brazilian Mixed Grill on a Skewer ... 126

C

Cala 105

Calzoni 47

Carbonada Criolla 119

Carpetbag Steak 59

Chaja 120

CHEESE
- Kesita 103
- Lasagne Imbottite 48
- Raclette 33
- Suppli di Riso 52

Chicken and Sweet Corn Soup 71

Chicken Satay 83

Chicken with Green Rice Singapura Inter Continental 86

Chicken Soup Tequendama Style 124

Chocolate Tartufo Tre Scalini 51

Cold Buttermilk Soup 23

Cold Chicken Wings with Brown Sauce 69

Copenhagen Salad 21

Cornets with Whipped Cream 21

Crab Soup 125

D

DESSERTS
- Banjo Pudding Dessert 100
- Bavarian Cream 30
- Bienmesabe 112
- Chaja 120
- Chocolate Tartufo Tre Scalini 51
- Cornets with Whipped Cream 21
- Devonshire Clotted Cream 39
- Dundee Cake 39

French Fruit Tart 43
Glazed Bananas 90
Guitar Cake 101
Karabeej 54
Papos de Anjo 128
Pavlova Southern Cross 62
Peach Embassy 26
Pear Dessert 30
Plum Pie 31
Summer Pudding 38
Suspiro Lemiño 116
Thai Crown of Fruit 64
Devonshire Clotted Cream 39
Dionysus Tart 10
Dried Mushrooms 72
Duck Cuzco 114
Dundee Cake 39
Dutch Fried Eggs 18
Dutch Koffie Tafel (Coffee Table) ... 14

E

EGGS
Dutch Fried Eggs 18
Eggs Cooked with Tea Leaves 76
Eggs in Gelatin 42
Veal, Ham and Egg Pie 40
Eggs in Gelatin 42
Eggs Cooked with Tea Leaves 76
Empanada Dough 130
Everyday Pancakes 16

F

Feijoada 127
Fiambre (Rolled Flank Steak) 118
Fillet of Sole Werner 29

FISH
Fillet of Sole Werner 29
Red Snapper 105
Steamboat 87
Sushi 97
Sweet and Sour Fish 77
Tarama 12
Tempura 95

FOWL
Chicken Satay 83
Chicken with Green Rice Singapura Inter Continental 86
Cold Chicken Wings with Brown Sauce 69
Dionysus Tart 10
Duck Cuzco 114
Fried Noodles with Assorted Meat. 69
Fried Rice with Assorted Meat 77
Galantine of Duck 36
Game Pie 38
Habash Mahshi (Stuffed Turkey) .. 56
Hajaccas 103
Puchero 129
Roast Chicken, Cantonese Style 92
Roast Duckling Gold Coast 61
Steamboat 87
Walnut Chicken 75
Yakitori 93
French Fruit Tart 43
Fried Noodles with Assorted Meat ... 69
Fried Rice with Assorted Meat 77
Fried Spring Rolls 88

G

Galantine of Duck 36
Game Pie 38
German Radish Salad 28
Glazed Bananas 90
Grilled Latin American Sausages 109
Guitar Cake 101

H

Habash Mahshi (Stuffed Turkey) 56
Hajaccas 103
HEARTY SANDWICHES
Calzoni 47
Mozzarella in Carroza 52
Hummus Bi Taheeni – Chick Peas with Sesame Oil 54

I

Irish Seafood Cocktail Inter Continental 25

K

Kabiss (Turnip Pickles) 58
Kaeng Phed (Meat Curry) 66
Karabeej 54
Katayef Phoenicia Inter Continental . 55
Keshy Yena Curacao Inter Continental 105
Kesita 103
Kung Nao (Shrimps in Winter) 65

L

LAMB
Brazilian Mixed Grill on a Skewer . 126
Lamb Las Trece Monedas 115
Mongolian Barbecue 89
Moussaka 11
Pie 'n' Sauce – Curried Lamb Pie .. 62
Roast Filet of Lamb Marfeuille 44

Souvlakia (Skewered Lamb) 12
Spit Roasted Lamb Mandarin Style . 74
Steamboat 87
Stuffed Vine Leaves 13
Lamb Las Trece Monedas 115
Lasagne Imbottite 48
Lentils Moudardara 58
Lobster Coral Bay 74
Lobster Curry, Lobster Plain 91
Lomo de Cerdo 124
Lumpia 82

M

Meat-Filled Pancake 15
Minced Veal Geneva Inter Continental 33
Mitzutaki 95
Mock Potato Rolls 17
Mongolian Barbecue 89
Moussaka 11
Mozzarella in Carroza 52
Mushroom Sauce 50

N

Neapolitan Sauce 49
Nut and Pâté Sandwiches 45

O

Onigiri (Rice Balls) 97
Onion Pie 35
Onion Soup 45

P

Pabellon 111
Palm Heart Salad 70
Papos de Anjo 128

PANCAKES
Everyday Pancakes 16
Katayef Phoenicia Inter Continental 55
Meat-Filled Pancakes 15
Real Holland Pancakes 16
Rusk Pancakes 17
Pancit 78
Pastechi 106
Pavlova Southern Cross 62
Pea Soup 18
Peach Embassy 26
Pear Desert 30
Peruvian Causa 113
Pesto Genovese 50
Picadinho 127
Pickled Mushrooms 41
Pie 'n' Sauce–Beef Pie 63
Pie 'n' Sauce–Curried Lamb Pie 62
Pineapple Bombay 99
Plum Pie 31

PORK
Bitterballen 15
Brazilian Mixed Grill on a Skewer .. 126
Dionysus Tart 10
Feijoada 127
Fried Noodles with Assorted Meat . 69
Fried Rice with Assorted Meat 77
Grilled Latin American Sausages .. 109
Hajaccas 103
Lomo de Cerdo 124
Lumpia 82
Mongolian Barbecue 89
Pancit 78
Pork Fillet Zio Mandy 74
Roast Ribs of Pork Siam
Inter Continental 66
Steamboat 87
Veal, Ham and Egg Pie 40
Pork Fillet Zio Mandy 74
Potato-Cheese Souffle 18
Potato Huancaina 114
Pu Cha (Stuffed Crab) 65
Puchero 129

R

Raclette 33
Real Holland Pancakes 16
Red Snapper 105
Roast Beef in Crust 34
Roast Chicken, Cantonese Style 92
Roast Duckling Gold Coast 61
Roast Filet of Lamb Marfeuille 44
Roast Ribs of Pork Siam
Inter Continental 66
Roquefort Roulades 76
Roquefort Sandwiches 45
Rusk Pancake 17

S

SALADS
Copenhagen Salad 21
German Radish Salad 28
Lentils Moudardara 58
Palm Heart Salad 70
Peruvian Causa 113
Potato Huancaina 114
Tabbouleh 53

SAUCES
Bolognese Sauce 49
Irish Seafood Cocktail
Inter Continental 25

Mushroom Sauce 50
Neapolitan Sauce 49
Pesto Genovese 50
Spaghetti Roquefort 122
Sauerbraten Frankfurt
Inter Continental 29

SHELLFISH
Baked Oysters Mornay 61
Carpetbag Steak 59
Fried Noodles with Assorted Meat . 69
Fried Rice with Assorted Meat 77
Kung Nao (Shrimps in Winter) 65
Lobster Coral Bay 74
Lobster Curry, Lobster Plain 91
Lumpia 82
Pancit 78
Pastechi 106
Pineapple Bombay 99
Pu Cha (Stuffed Crab) 65
Shrimp Brochette Victoria Plaza 122
Shrimp Chow Chow 10
Shrimps Bahamas 73
Shrimps Tassia 11
Steamboat 87
Tempura 95
Ukoy Shrimp Fritter 80
Shrimp Brochette Victoria Plaza 122
Shrimp Chow Chow 10
Shrimps Bahamas 73
Shrimps Tassia 11
Smorrebrod 23
Sobrebarriga 123
Sopito 106

SOUPS
Avgolemono Soup 9
Chicken and Sweet Corn Soup 71
Chicken Soup Tequendama Style ... 124
Cold Buttermilk Soup 23
Crab Soup 125
Onion Soup 45
Pea Soup 18
Sopito 106
Souvlakia (Skewered Lamb) 12
Spaghetti Roquefort 122
Spinach Pie 47
Spit Roasted Lamb Mandarin Style .. 74
Steamboat 87
Stuffed Vine Leaves 13
Sukiyaki Okura 94
Summer Pudding 38
Suppli Di Riso 52
Sushi 97
Suspiro Lemiño 116
Sweet and Sour Fish 77

T

Tabbouleh 53
Tamanaco Carne Asado 110
Tarama 12
Tempura 95
Teppan-Yaki 94
Thai Crown of Fruit 64
Tostados 109
Turkish Onions 42

U

Ukoy Shrimp Fritter 80

V

VEAL
Anticuchos Mixed Peruvian Grill ... 116
Bitterballen 15
Carbonada Criolla 119
Minced Veal Geneva
Inter Continental 33
Veal Cutlets Kublai Khan 70
Veal, Ham and Egg Pie 40
Veal Cutlets Kublai Khan 70
Veal, Ham and Egg Pie 40

VEGETABLES
Bavarian Potato Dumplings 28
Dried Mushrooms 72
Mock Potato Rolls 17
Onion Pie 35
Peruvian Causa 113
Pickled Mushrooms 41
Potato-Cheese Souffle 18
Spinach Pie 47
Turkish Onions 42
Zuurkool Met Spek 17

W

Walnut Chicken 75

Y

Yakitori 93

Z

Zuurkool Met Spek 17